Saint, Martyr, Virgin, Slave

Faith and Freedom Forever

Second Edition

Saint, Martyr, Virgin, Slave

Faith and Freedom Forever

Second Edition

Heroic Stories Based on Historical Records

EDWARD N BROWN

CRYSTAL SEA PRESS
CHICAGO, IL

SAINT, MARTYR, VIRGIN, SLAVE
Faith and Freedom Forever
Second Edition

Copyright © 2024 by Edward N Brown

ISBN: 978-1-7367712-0-4
Library of Congress Control Number: 2021904294

Published by Crystal Sea Press, Chicago, IL
CSP
Printed in the United States of America

For information about this title, or to order other books and/or electronic media, contact the publisher at: www.crystalseapress.com

They were marginalized, denigrated, and persecuted

But they valued Faith and Freedom above all

These are the stories of the unsung heroes – remarkable women of unbelievable strength, courage, and virtue – who gave up their lives for their faith and their freedom – who found eternal love, peace, and joy as saints in heaven.

The holy women martyrs – young and old –
married and unmarried – slave and free
they climbed the highest ladder and paid the highest price – they must not be forgotten.

Note to the Reader:
Similar stories continue today in many different forms and disguises – some subtle, some severe – as new and malicious vilifications against faith and freedom continuously rear up all over the world.

Let the past be both a comfort and a warning!
Assaults on faith and freedom, under all sorts of pretenses, are here and now – and will not go away. The saints in heaven bear witness, and the saints on earth are accountable.

Vigilance is key!
Heroes will rise to resist the threats against faith and freedom.
Are you one of them?

CONTENTS

PREFACE

THE book in your hand is not a history book or a modern-day inspirational. Rather, it is a collection of stories, yarns, and snippets, based on actual historical records, of events that challenged the spiritual fortitude of the very first Christians – their freedom and their faith – as well as the perseverance of the Christian religion itself. As such, it is both documentary and encouragement in nature. The purpose is to REMEMBER, COMPREHEND, APPRECIATE, and LEARN from past events and long-forgotten marginalized people.

Many of these individuals have become saints – evangelists, heroes, founders, benefactors, ascetics – but the heroic female saints, in particular, are represented in this volume. And it is the martyrs – virgin martyrs and slave martyrs – that are particularly remembered here. Human beings who sacrificed it all for their freedom and their faith – and individuals within our culture that have not always been given full recognition and respect.

The time period of interest is the first 300 years (more or less) after the death and resurrection of Jesus Christ, although many similar assaults on freedom, faith, and human dignity have been repeated throughout all history – and continue to this day in various forms and disguises – some subtle, some severe. The hope is that by remembering crucial events from the past, and empathizing with the heroic figures therefrom, it will light up our spiritual awareness, and strengthen our resolve to always maintain a vigilance against threats that can affect our future contentment. Because the freedom to willingly put one's faith in Jesus Christ, is the only way to salvation and eternal happiness.

Today's issues of racism and women's rights are the modern outgrowths of ancient injustices. The early Christian church was not trying to revolutionize secular society, but it had a major influence on how women (especially slaves and young unmarried women) viewed their roles in life. Their stories must be told so that we can learn from history, and apply that knowledge appropriately to the issues being faced today.

INTRODUCTION

In the Roman Catholic and Eastern Orthodox religious traditions, all people in heaven are considered to be saints. But some deserve special recognition for having lived lives of great holiness and virtue. These people are singled out and formally acknowledged for their 'heroic sanctity' – they are revered by the Church as having attained an honored place in heaven. They are a diverse group of people with varied and unusual stories. Their ranks include kings and queens, peasants, missionaries, ascetics, evangelists, theologians, workers, parents, children of all ages, nuns, priests, and 'everyday folks' who dedicated their lives to the loving pursuit of God. It also includes the martyrs and the slaves – people who put their faith and freedom above everything else.

In the 10th century, Pope John XV formalized a canonization process for the identification of saints. Before that time, saints were largely established by popular demand – when the degree of public arousal and adoration was high (spontaneous public attribution).[1] Today, there are more than 10,000 saints recognized by the Roman Catholic Church alone, though the names and stories of many of these holy men and women have been lost to history.[2]

Among the Eastern Orthodox and Oriental Orthodox traditions, the number is very intractable since there is no fixed process of 'canonization', and each individual jurisdiction within the two Orthodox traditions independently maintains parallel lists of saints that have only partial overlap (the Roman Catholic, Eastern Orthodox, Oriental Orthodox, Anglican Communion, and various Lutheran churches venerate some saints unique to their own traditions). The Coptic church also preserves their own list of martyrs and saints. The number of saints that are honored in all the various Christian traditions is certainly greater than 10,000, but obtaining an exact count is basically impossible. Many are listed as just members of a group and are nameless; and groups often have an inaccurate or exaggerated number of members. Other persons are duplicated under different names. Others have made-up names, and others have very little creditable evidence to support an actual life, rather than just pure myth. Curiously, Catholic lists of saints often also include angels and archangels (although only a small number). A comprehensive list of all saints is a massive undertaking, but a good start can be found online at Wikipedia, Catholic Online, and Britannica.[3]

In this book, the focus of interest is on female martyrs in the years prior to 313 AD, the year in which the Christians were guaranteed freedom to practice their religion by the Edict of Milan, under Roman emperor Constantine the Great. Of particular interest are the martyrs who were also slaves, the people at the very bottom of the social strata, whose stories are both tragic and sad, but illustrate their stamina and determination to win freedom. The virgin martyrs are also highlighted, as many of their stories are both heartbreaking and distressing, reflecting the norms of the time. They desired freedom from arranged marriages and imposed childbirth and child-rearing. Both the slave martyrs and the virgin martyrs were richly honored by the early church – their stories are touching and moving – their strength and courage were immeasurable – their faith unwavering – and they provided a bit of hope and solace to a fallen world.

The number of unmarried young women martyrs who have been personally identified as a slave is somewhere around 10, but there are many shades of gray here (e.g., distinction between servants and slaves, indentured and contracted, tradition and circumstance, etc.), so the number is very imprecise. Furthermore, such members of large consolidated group martyrdoms are lost to examination. Very little is known about these forgotten heroes. Their quest for both spiritual and physical freedom was unimaginable to most people today. Marginalized, denigrated, and persecuted, they climbed the highest ladder of all. They truly were of the greatest holiness and virtue, and deserve to be remembered and acknowledged for their 'heroic sanctity' by those of us still on our earthly journey.

ORGANIZATION

AFTER providing the background setting of historical persecution against Christians, particularly against women, slaves, and unmarried maidens, a more in-depth analysis is presented of just who the persecuted people really were – where they came from, what they did, and where they wanted to go. Following this are the stories of the heroic martyrs – the exalted heroes followed by the stories of the unmarried (virgins), the slaves, and the unmarried slaves. Stories of the lesser heroes are in the next chapter.[4] Commentary and Appendices (containing a detailed list of all names) complete the main content of the book.

The stories are based on historical records,[5] but the exact degree of ultimate truth in each story is uncertain because of the uncertain veracity of the author of the accounts, and the manner (and integrity) of preservation (oral tradition, letter, document, etc.).[6] Each story provides a first-hand accounting of events that actually transpired, resulting in severe persecution of Christians, and the martyrdom of one or more heroic figures.

The Stories of the Exalted Heroes

The telling of the stories of Blandina, Perpetua and Felicitas, and the three sisters, Agape, Chionia, and Irene, are in the form of a letter to the religious faithful, by a person close to the action, but not sufficiently close so as to be lumped in with the persecuted group of believers. The letter-writer probably felt some shame in not being able to witness to the level of ultimate sacrifice, and that he had to hide himself under the cover of anonymity (since there was a real possibility that the letter would be intercepted and traced back to the originator – with a high likelihood of extreme repercussions – the writer had to know this, had reconciled himself to the possibility, and was prepared to face the consequences), but he was sufficiently motivated out of love and compassion (both for the people involved and for the faith) to put pen-to-paper and send out a correspondence that the authorities would probably consider inflammatory.[7]

The three stories are at different points in time and at different geographic locations, so it was not the same letter-writer. In reality, each letter-writer was in a different circumstance with different motivations and different persuasions. In addition to the details of the event, the introductory paragraph of the letter would be different in each case based upon the time, place, mood, and background surroundings. However, to avoid a repetitive beginning to each chapter, the letter has been removed from the beginning of each. A generic letter has been created that is equally applicable to all stories, and improves the readability by removing repetitiveness of the chapter opening.

Therefore, the reader should view the three stories as a narrative (in the form of a letter) from a captivated bystander, of a real-life sequence of events, that has been written with the intent to make sure that others become aware of these events, and that they are never forgotten. It is a letter that tells a story from the heart – a story of unbelievable cruelty by men to their fellow human beings – but at the same time, a story of immense personal faith and fortitude by virtuous individuals, and their commitment to their faith under the most deplorable circumstances – a story that truly illustrates both the very worst and also the very best of qualities of the human condition.

SALUTATION AND OPENING OF A LETTER TO THE FAITHFUL

To the bishops, deacons, presbyters, and devoted believers in the holy churches of Rome, Alexandria, Antioch, and Jerusalem; and to the faithful brothers and sisters in all the holy churches scattered throughout Asia, Macedonia, Palestine, Africa, Greece, and Italy:

From an anonymous and humbled servant of our Lord Jesus Christ, fearful of persecution and saddened by the horrific events of the past few days, but determined to preserve the memories of our most holy saints, and to record the truth of what actually happened here unaltered by official reports or unofficial scurrilous slanders:

I write to you with heavy heart, but with conviction that the love of our most holy God and Lord Jesus Christ will overcome the evil that has tormented us, and that the wicked will be forgiven their sins and the heathen will be saved and baptized. I look forward to the day when all souls will live in harmony with God.

But today I am saddened beyond words. Although the path to salvation and resurrection is rocky, and there are many followers of the 'evil one' ready to cause hurt and despair, the Light of our Lord is still bright – and many good souls are prepared to make the ultimate sacrifice for the faith, just as Jesus of Nazareth did. They will be glorified in heaven, but their names and lives should also be remembered here on earth. We must not forget them. As holy saints, they can help us in our quest for righteousness, and our hopes for eternal salvation, peace, and glory with God the Father, the Holy Spirit, and Christ Jesus our Lord.

As such, the events that occurred here, and to which I now relate by my hand, along with the names of the holy souls who sacrificed everything in defense of our most sacred faith, must not be forgotten. The world needs to know and remember what happened here. May the martyrs rest in peace forever.

NOTES

---

1. In 1969, Pope Paul VI created the 'Congregation for the Causes of Saints' to oversee and validate the canonization process. He also suppressed several older saints' venerations largely on the basis that the attributed acts, miracles, and even basic facts of their existence, could not be verified with any reasonable degree of certainty (however, people already under their patronage could continue to venerate them, but they would no longer appear on the Roman calendar, and no new parishes or other institutions could open under their name).

2. The precise number of Catholic saints will always be debatable. Early Christian communities venerated hundreds of saints, but historical research by 17th- and 18th-century Catholic scholars determined that very few of these saints' stories were backed by solid historical evidence. Nevertheless, there have been thousands of canonizations in modern times. Pope John Paul II alone canonized 110 individuals, as well as many group canonizations such as 110 martyr saints of China, 103 Korean martyrs, 117 Vietnamese martyrs, the Mexican Martyrs, Spanish martyrs, and French revolutionary martyrs. On May 12, 2013 Pope Francis recognized another 802 saints – one from Colombia, one from Mexico, and 800 residents of Otranto in southern Italy, killed for refusing to convert to Islam after Ottoman Turks besieged their town in 1480 (The Martyrs of Otronto).

3. Check out https://en.wikipedia.org/wiki/List_of_saints; https://en.wikipedia.org/wiki/Chronological_list_of_saints_and_blesseds; http://www.gcatholic.org/saints/index.htm; https://www.britannica.com/topic/list-of-saints-2061264.

4. Please note that the lesser heroes are not 'lesser' in divine importance, nor even in earthly historical impact/importance. They just have ended up with reduced substantiating information, and lesser widespread dissemination, lobbying weight, and hype. The exalted heroes simply make for a better story. In reality, from the standpoint of salvation and everlasting life, whether icon or minion, all sincere saints and martyrs are equal in the eyes of God.

5. Refer to the following for more detailed information:

Herbert Musurillo, *The Acts of the Christian Martyrs* [Oxford: University Press, 1972]

Anthony Schiavo, Jr. (ed.), *I am a Christian: Authentic Accounts of Christian Martyrdom and Persecution from the Ancient Sources* [Merchantville, NJ: ARX Publishing, 2018]

6. In addition, certain literary license was invoked in order to dramatize the story for emotional effect, by both the historical author and the present author.

7. Of course, this is not meant to imply that the letter-writer was male – it could just as readily have been a female writer.

1 BACKGROUND SETTING

After the Resurrection and Ascension

S hortly after the death, resurrection, and ascension of Jesus and the coming of the Holy Spirit, the apostles Peter and John begin to openly preach the Good News to the Jews in Jerusalem, boldly and confidently. Their message?

The Almighty God of the Universe has ordained that the man from Nazareth named Jesus, who has been crucified on the hill of Golgotha,[1] is in Truth the Lord and Messiah, as predicted by the prophets – and that through sincere belief in Him, repentant sins can be forgiven, and people can be resurrected from death and achieve everlasting life.

The Good News is that God has given us a new covenant, one that puts the old covenants with Noah, Abraham, and Moses, in a new perspective – one that is full of grace and provides real hope for all people.

On the day of Pentecost, following a riveting sermon by Peter, 3000 people are baptized in the name of Jesus Christ. The year is 33 AD.[2] The 'Christian' movement – at first known as 'The Way'[3] – has started, although it is not until a few years later that the believers are first called 'Christians'.[4]

In the following days, Peter and John testify to the crowds in the temple under Solomon's Portico (Colonnade)[5] and heal

11

a crippled beggar at the gate, converting many into believers and disciples. In less than two months, through a combination of selected healing and earnest preaching, the 'Christian' movement grows to about 5000 men, not counting family members. And this growth spurt catches the attention of the 70-member Jewish governing council, known as the Sanhedrin, that had just recently tried Jesus and sentenced him to death through deft political maneuvering. But the 'church' of Jesus Christ has officially begun.[6]

The high priests of the temple, particularly the Sadducees,[7] are annoyed and irritated by this growing movement. Identified as the chief agitators, Peter and John are briefly brought before the high council of the Sanhedrin, and subsequently are arrested and put in the public prison.[8] When confronted face-to-face the next day, they exclaim:

The God of our ancestors raised up Jesus, whom you had killed by hanging him on a cross. God exalted him at his right hand as Leader and Savior, that he might give repentance to Israel and forgiveness of sins. And we are witnesses to these things, and so is the Holy Spirit whom God has given to those who obey him.[9]

When the priests on the council hear this, they are disturbed and consider it the worst kind of blasphemy. They are so angry, that they want to kill the two apostles. But a respected Pharisee in the council named Gamaliel provides some relief by admonishing the apostles and then convincing the high priests that a stern warning, accompanied by a good flogging, would be sufficient to shut them up.

Of course, it doesn't work. Every day thereafter, Peter, John, and all the apostles, continue to teach and proclaim Jesus as the Messiah both in the temple and from house to house throughout the city.

To help with the logistics and accounts, the believers of

'The Way'[10] select seven disciples of good standing (known simply as 'The Seven') in order to allow the apostles more time for prayer and preaching.[11] One of the men chosen is named Stephen, and he is full of grace and faith. By the power of the Holy Spirit, he exuberantly testifies for the Lord by performing many signs and wonders among the people.

But many of the Jews are irritated (especially those from Asia and Africa) and vehemently argue against him. They accuse him of speaking sacrilege against Moses, David, and Solomon. They quickly gather a sympathetic following – and finally, they can bear no more. Stirring up the supporters, scribes, and elders, they confront him, seize him, and then bring him before the council, accusing him of claiming that the Jesus movement was going to destroy the temple and revise the traditions of Moses.[12] In his defense, Stephen says,

I see the heavens opened and the Son of Man standing at the right hand of God.[13]

This was the last straw – the council members become enraged, and together with the temple police and officials, have him dragged out of the city to a rocky patch of scrub land nearby – where unruly mob behavior prevails; and Stephen is stoned to death – all while forgiving them with his last gasping words.[14] Minding (watching over) the fine coats of the attackers, as they carried out the dirty sweaty work of gathering up and hurling the hefty stones, is a young man named Saul. A learned traditionalist, he has no patience or tolerance for members of this new movement (also sometimes called the 'Jesus cult', or 'cult of the Nazarene') and impassively endorses the killing of Stephen.[15]

On this day in the year 36 AD, the deadly persecution of Christians and the Christian church begins – and make no mistake about it, severe persecution continues actively to this very day.

NOTES

---

1. Golgotha means 'skull' in Hebrew. The native Roman Latin word is Calvary. People call the place 'skull' because it's the city's execution site outside the walls, it more-or-less looks like a skull, and it is near some local tombs.

2. Jimmy Akin, National Catholic Register, 10 April 2020, https://www.ncregister.com/

3. The Christians got this name for their religious movement because they believed that Jesus was the only way to the Father, as evidenced by when He said, *I am the way, and the truth, and the life. No one comes to the Father except through me.* (John 14:6). Refer also to Acts 9:2 and Acts 11:26.

4. The nickname 'Christian' (which may have originally been akin to an insult) started in Antioch, Syria, where Barnabas was pastor of a church of Greek and Hebrew Jews. Eventually, the new name stuck, and the former designation, believers in 'The Way', faded into obscurity.

5. Solomon's Colonnade was a wall of the outer courtyard of the temple, where both Jews and non-Jews were allowed to congregate. It was covered with a cedar roof and stretched 300 yards long. This is where the very first Christians first met for worship.

6. In actuality, the 'church' officially began with Jesus' declaration in Matthew 16:18, *And so I tell you Peter: you are a rock, and on this rock foundation I will build my church, and the forces of Hell will not prevail against it.*

7. The Sadducees were mainly the priests and the social influential elite. They felt bound only to the laws of Moses, and not the hundreds of extra laws (detailed specifics) that the Pharisees had added. The Pharisees, on the other hand, were oppressively legalistic, insisting that all their added extra laws were just as important as the laws of Moses. The Sadducees believed in God, but rejected the immortality of the soul, the resurrection of the body, and the existence of angels and spirits.

8. During that night, Peter and John were freed by an angel of God, and instructed to continue preaching in the temple. This they did the very next morning, surprising the priests and council members who thought that they were incarcerated. Temple police were dispatched to round them up and bring them back into the council chambers, where they were interrogated by the high priest. See Acts 5:19-28.

9. Acts 5:30-32

10. Believers of 'The Way' were followers of the 'Christian' movement – primarily Jews who maintained that the Messiah had come, and his name was Jesus – see Endnote #3.

11. The loose association to which the believers belonged (then called 'The Way' by the believers, but now more commonly referred to as the fledgling church of Jesus Christ), had a compassionate ministry program that included providing food for needy people, such as widows. The responsibility for this was delegated to the seven chosen disciples – Stephen, Philip (the Evangelist [or the deacon]), Prochorus, Nicanor, Timon, Parmenas, and Nicolaus – after complaints by Greek-speaking Jews that their widows weren't getting as much food as the Hebrew-speaking widows (the local favorites).

12. For many years, non-believers referred to the worship of Jesus, and the following of His ways, as the 'Jesus movement' or 'Jesus cult'. Gentiles (particularly the Romans) considered it as a fringe sect within Judaism.

13. Acts 7:56

14. Acts 7:59-60

15. Saul is his Hebrew name. But he is better known by his Greek name – Paul – the man who will become Christianity's most famous convert, and write almost half the books of the New Testament.

2 THE PERSECUTIONS

From 33 to 313 AD

In short order, Saul and the Jewish religious police start a round-up of believers, disciples, followers, and supporters by going house-to-house, dragging out both men and women suspects, and sending them off to interrogation centers and prisons (when thought appropriate).[1] The persecution is harsh and relentless. Fearful of loss of life, health, property, or reputation, the ruthless violence and harassment drive many good people out of Jerusalem. The apostles hunker down in secret rooms in private homes, but most other believers leave town altogether and scatter throughout the countryside of Judea, Samaria, and beyond.[2] But wherever they go, they take their new faith with them and proclaim the 'Good News' of 'The Way'. Churches are set up clandestinely, and very quickly, the teachings of Jesus spread all over the Roman Empire.[3] But trouble is lurking.

The first apostle to leave Jerusalem was Philip. He traveled to the town of Samaria (the main town in the region of Samaria) and began to preach the 'Good News', in accordance with the final directive of Jesus.[4] He was well received by the people and performed many miracle healings and exorcisms. In the town was a charlatan named Simon

Magus, who was very popular among the gullible and unaware, because of the phony magic and sham sorcery that he used to trick and bewitch them with. He pretended to believe in Philip's message,[5] but he just wanted to learn Philip's 'magic' so that he could benefit from it himself. When Peter and John arrived to bring the Holy Spirit, through the laying on of hands, Simon revealed his true unholy nature and was severely rebuked by Peter. But Simon did not honestly repent. He continued to practice his swindles, even incorporating some of the words and sayings of the infant church.[6] This was the beginning of another form of threat and persecution against the Word of God. Imitators, false messiahs, self-proclaimed saviors, and purveyors of twisted belief would plague the believers of 'The Way' for many years. Although usually not deadly, the net effect of such heretical movements was of great concern to the fledgling church. And a by-product of this oppression, that presented a real physical threat, was the industry that surrounded the movement. Physicians lamenting their lack of business, and idol-makers lamenting their lack of sales, could present real problems, as the disciples and apostles would soon learn.[7]

From the beginning of the 'Christian' movement, women were prominent among those who suffered for their faith, as evidenced by Saul's campaign against the believers in 'The Way'. He gets authorization from the high temple priest to arrest and bring to Jerusalem anyone that he finds in Damascus, man or woman, living according to 'The Way' (what he sarcastically calls the 'new way').[8] Women were not exempted. In the eyes of Saul, they were just as guilty as men in desecrating the Jewish faith. How many were killed or beleaguered by Saul and other Jewish dogmatists, we will never know. The fact that almost all believers and disciples left Jerusalem at this time, testifies to the harshness of the oppression. But the Jewish harassment and discrimination, coupled with vexation by purveyors of twisted belief (and their backers with vested interests) was just the beginning of antagonism and hostility directed toward Christian believers. State-sponsored persecution loomed ahead.

FIRST CENTURY PERSECUTION

IN 52 AD, the Roman emperor Claudius ordered the expulsion of all Jews from Rome because of turmoil resulting from clashes between followers and antagonists of a certain man called Christus (at this time, the Jesus movement was considered a sub-cult of the Jewish religion by the Romans).[9] The biblical personages Priscilla and Aquila left Rome and emigrated to Corinth under this decree, where they met up with the Apostle Paul shortly thereafter. The Roman rulers now knew that an underground movement was afoot within the Jewish people that fostered deep divisions.[10] This complicated the political landscape. However, as more and more Gentiles began to embrace this new sect, it became apparent that, in actuality, a new religion had emerged – a new religion with a host of new problems for the empire. Dealing exclusively with the Jews would no longer be sufficient. Now they would have to deal with a new cult – one growing rapidly among the Gentiles – with strange customs and activities – and one that presented a whole new bunch of challenges – the Christians.

First Martyrs of the Church of Rome

Some 20 years after Saul's torment, during the reign of the Roman Emperor Nero, a fiery conflagration razed much of Rome. There is ample speculation as to exactly how the fire started, but to divert attention from the privileged classes and find a quick scapegoat, the Christians were forthrightly blamed. There were already many Christians in Rome within a dozen or so years after the death of Jesus,[11] though they were not the converts of Paul, since he had not yet visited Rome. Some were Jewish and some were Gentile, but they had all heard the 'Good News' through word-of-mouth, emanating from the wandering 70 disciples and the many people in Judea and Samaria who had been personally affected by Jesus' ministry. Many people were rounded up suspecting to be Christian – rich and poor – and many were tortured or killed. Many 'ratted' on the Christians, but many held firm to their convictions.[12] The intensity of persecution continued in rippling waves in the city, and throughout the empire, for years.[13] Again, women were not exempted. The fact that women were significantly represented in the persecutions clearly shows that they were active participants in the movement, and not just innocent wives, daughters, and hangers-on.

Identified as the 'First Martyrs of the Church of Rome',[14] these were Christians who were martyred during emperor Nero's persecution in 64 AD and shortly thereafter, in retaliation for their starting (which he alleged) the 'great fire of 64'.[15] Widespread rumor had blamed the tragedy on the unpopular emperor Nero, who wanted to enlarge his palace and was looking for an excuse to do so. He in turn, passed the buck, and accused the Christians, who he said were "infamous for their abominations."[16] The persecution was quick and severe. The rationale for the denunciation of the Christians went something like this:

> The origin of the name 'Christian' comes from a man who was called 'Christ'. He was executed as a criminal by the Roman governor Pontius Pilate during the reign of emperor Tiberius. Although repressed, this destructive superstition has erupted again, not only throughout Judea, which was the origin of this

evil, but also within the city of Rome, to which all that is horrible and shameful floods together and is strangely celebrated.

Public outcry was minimal when Nero ordered thousands to be executed with the most exquisite punishments. Using the information extracted from the first members who were seized and tortured (some of them probably being slaves), a vast multitude of Christians were rounded-up and convicted, not so much for the crime of starting the fire, but for being 'horrible and shameful human beings who had a hatred for the goodness of the human race' (the publicized denouncement). Some of those convicted were covered with the skins of animals and thrown to wild dogs or wolves to be torn apart. Others were crucified, and at sunset were slathered with oil or wax, tied to posts, and then burned alive – human torches whose glow illuminated Nero's garden parties and lit the path of his chariots. Nero flaunted his ostentatious nature by presenting the spectacle in the amphitheatre, as if it was a sport, while he mingled with the people in the dress of a charioteer as he swaggered about the place. At least 574 individual martyrs have been recognized by the Catholic church, but the exact number is of course unknown.

Among those martyred were the grand apostles, Peter and Paul.[17] What is not widely known, however, is that Peter's wife was martyred just shortly before he met his fate. As it turns out, she was doing much more than merely shopping and sightseeing in the big city – she was not a simple bystander to her husband's ministry. Rather, she was a bona fide threat to the Roman order in her own right. Her faithfulness to Jesus and His church cost her everything, yet the church barely recognizes her devotion. Seeing his own wife led away to execution, Peter cried out to her in a consolatory but encouraging voice, addressing her by name,[18] and exhorting her to "remember the Lord!"[19] Such was the marriage of this blessed saint and his blessed wife. To the end, they were one with each other, and one with the Lord.[20]

Included in those martyred were 47 believers baptized by Peter, and three Roman soldiers who converted to the faith after undergoing a profound and moving spiritual experience while witnessing the martyrdom of Paul (for this crime, they were condemned and executed).

The Holy Monastic Martyr Eudokia

Born in 21 AD in Samaria, Eudokia was an attractive young woman who lived in the city of Heliopolis in Phoenicia.[21] However, she was an idolater and led a licentious life. Stunningly beautiful, she had many wealthy lovers, led many people into sin, and amassed a great fortune therefrom. As a harlot, she never considered the judgement of her soul after death – her soul was deadened and her heart hardened.

She learned about Christianity from a monk by the name of Germanus, who was returning to his monastery from a pilgrimage.[22] Suffering from an illness, she awoke one night at midnight and heard singing from the house of a Christian woman next door. Germanus was reading from a book which described the Last Judgment,[23] the punishment of sinners, and the reward of the righteous; and the woman was softly singing in the background. The grace of God touched Eudokia's heart, and she grieved because of her great wealth and for her sinful life.

In the morning, Eudokia hastened to call on the man whose prayer she had heard the previous night. She listened a long time to his guidance, and her soul was filled with joy and love for Christ. She wanted to believe, but it all sounded too good to be true. "Could she also be saved?" she asked. Germanus told her to remain alone in her room for one week, fasting and praying – and that she would receive a vision which would assure her of God's love for her.

And indeed, it was true – the archangel Michael appeared to her and showed her the wonders and mercy of God. In her vision, Michael was leading her to heaven while many angels were rejoicing. She also saw a shadowy figure howling and moaning because he had been cheated out of a soul. That very day, Eudokia confessed Christ as the one True God. At the end of the week, Germanus told her to give away her wealth and to put her previous life behind her – and she received holy baptism from bishop Theodotus of Heliopolis.

Eudokia was 30 years old when she gave herself over completely to the service of the Lord. The year was 51 AD. Her first act was to help build a monastery near Heliopolis, where she administered the disposition of her wealth to projects for charity. She took upon herself strict acts of penitence, and in a short time, the monastery became a beacon which attracted thousands of spiritually starved people. The Lord granted her forgiveness, and endowed her with spiritual gifts. Eudokia soon became famous for the beauty of her soul, acquiring in the process of her noble work, a proximity to God no riches could ever buy.

After she had become the mother superior of the monastery, a young pagan man, named Philostrates (one of her former lovers), heard of her conversion to Christ and longed to see her again in the hope of securing favor before her fortune had been dissipated. Aflame with impious passion, he came into the monastery in the guise of a monk, and began to urge Eudokia to return to Heliopolis and resume her former life. But Eudokia sharply rebuked him, and he fell down dead at her feet. As she was kneeling down trying to administer to him, the Lord appeared to her in a vision and said, "Arise, Eudokia, and pray for the resurrection of the dead man." And so she did – and so it was. Philostrates was restored to life, and begged the nun to forgive him. He was baptized, returned to Heliopolis, and never forgot the mercy of God and holiness of Eudokia.

When persecutions against Christians intensified, they arrested Eudokia and brought her to governor Diogenes to be tried. During the trial, the military commander Diodorus received news of the sudden death of his wife Firmina. In despair, he rushed to Eudokia with a plea to pray for his departed wife and restore her to life. Filled with great faith, Eudokia turned to God with prayer and supplication, and asked for a return of Firmina's life. And through the power and grace of the Lord, Firmina was returned, and Diodorus and Diogenes became believers in Christ and were baptized together with their families.

Eudokia performed other wondrous miracles during her time in the monastery, where she lived for 56 years.

After Diogenes died the new governor was Vicentius, a fierce persecutor of Christians. Having learned of the accomplishments of the Christian nun, he gave orders to execute her. The holy martyr Eudokia was beheaded in 107 AD at the age of 86.

Saint Matthew and Ephigenia

Raised from the dead, converted to Christianity, and consecrated to God by Saint Matthew the Apostle, Ephigenia was the eldest daughter of Egippus,[24] the king of 'Ethiopia' (the slang term used for the regions southwest of the Caspian Sea, either in northern Mesopotamia or in Ancient Armenia).[25] By the miracle of raising Ephigenia from the dead, king Egippus was converted to Christianity, and the Faith was spread throughout the ancient land.

Ephigenia had consecrated her virginity to God after having frequently heard Matthew preach on the priceless value of purity, and urging people to guard and preserve it.

Her example was followed by many other young women, who, choosing the princess as their mother superior, lived together and occupied their time in prayer and spiritual work.

However, when Hirtacus succeeded Egippus as king, he desired for Ephigenia to become his wife. But she wasn't interested in marriage and shunned the king. Undeterred, he promised Matthew half of his kingdom if he could persuade Ephigenia to marry him. So, Matthew invited the king to Mass the following Sunday, where he explained to him that she was already married to the eternal God and King in heaven, and therefore could not be married to anyone else. Enraged and affronted by this, the king sent a swordsman to kill Matthew. While standing at the church altar and still sermonizing about God, the swordsman burst in and mercilessly carried out his order. The great Apostle Matthew had become a heroic martyr for Christ. The year was 68 AD.

Not having managed to bend Ephigenia to his will, Hirtacus tried to destroy her home with fire. But the flames miraculously turned away from the house, and instead enveloped the royal palace. The king's son was seized by the devil, and the king himself contracted leprosy, eventually killing himself. Ephigenia lived an ascetic life, peacefully fostering the spread of the Gospel.

Persecution in the Roman Empire

Those who followed the religious teachings of Jesus were sought out as enemies of Rome – unbelievers in the Roman gods and unwilling to accept the divinity of the emperor.[26] From Nero until the recognition of Christianity by the Emperor Constantine the Great in 313 AD (the Edict of Milan) and the designation of Christianity (Nicene Christianity) as the official state religion by emperor Theodosius I in 380 AD (the Edict of Thessalonica),[27] there were sporadic persecutions of Christians – some of them very severe – for over 250 years. Throughout this period, women and men alike chose to die rather than renounce their faith in Christ. Some died alone; others died with their companions in round-ups of believer congregates.

When Christianity first began, it was seen as a fringe sect within Judaism, but before long Christians were bringing attention to themselves by their aloofness, and 'secret' activities. There were rumors and gossips of 'eating flesh' (cannibalism)[28] and other surmised abnormal behaviors (sexual orgies and incest were often alleged). Their aloofness brought criticism of their anti-social behavior (along with veiled threats of treason), and when things went wrong in society, Christians began to be singled out as the culprits. But failure to worship the emperor and the gods quickly became the trump card of the oppressors. The Christians were to blame for every public disaster and every misfortune that befell the people. Whether flood, drought, earthquake, famine, or plague, the cry to send the 'Christians to the lions' would inevitably arise. In the earliest attested martyrology, the death of Saint Ignatius of Rome is said to have occurred sometime between 98 and 117 AD.

SECOND CENTURY PERSECUTION

IN 107 AD, the emperor Trajan hosted four solid months of public spectacle games at Rome's Colosseum (also known as the Flavian Amphitheatre) to celebrate his victories over the barbarians in Dacia (modern-day Romania) and incorporating the province into the empire.[29] In addition to gladiatorial contests, the Colosseum was used to stage animal shows, executions, historical dramas, and re-enactments of famous victorious battles.[30] Executions were a common feature of the Roman games. They took place around midday as an interlude between the animal shows of the morning session and the combat spectacle in the afternoon.[31] The executions of army deserters, prisoners-of-war, and criminals from the lower classes were normally carried out as burnings, beheadings, crucifixions, or damnation by beasts (where they would face tormented and hungry wild animals), the choice determined by severity of crime and social class.[32]

Such events were occasionally on a huge scale. The games under Trajan involved 11,000 animals (most of which were killed) and 10,000 gladiators over the course of 123 days. Many executions were staged at midday. If not crucified, beheaded, or burned alive, those condemned to death would be sent into the arena, naked and unarmed, to face the beasts of death which would literally tear them to pieces. That particular spectacle was popular with many of the baser spectators.[33] Although there are no extant records to reveal the administrative, demographic, econometric, or sociologic data pertinent to the executions, it is certain that some Christians (and probably some women and some slaves) were included in these games of terror.[34]

When Trajan was informed about the problem of the Christians (how and why they behaved the way they did), and asked what should be done about them, his response was that they should not be sought out after, but if and when found, they should be punished. This somewhat lessoned the persecutions which had been threatening to erupt and boil over. But there were still plenty of pretexts left for those citizens and officials who disliked the Christians and wanted them to disappear. In various places, plots would be staged to seek out and round up suspected Christians, trump up horrible accusations, charge them with various ridiculous crimes, and exact penalties and punishments on those who would not disavow and repudiate the cult. Although no great persecution took place for a while, local persecutions were nevertheless going on in particular provinces, and many of the believers endured martyrdom in various forms.

There were a number of martyrs around 150 AD, including that of the famous Christian presbyter Polycarp, the bishop of the church at Smyrna,[35] and first person to be associated with the term 'Catholic church'. Polycarp died a martyr in 155 AD,[36] bound and burned at the stake, then stabbed to death when the fire failed to consume his body. He was probably the last surviving person to have known an apostle, having been a disciple of Saint John. The church at Smyrna was compared to a 'Catholic church' by Saint Ignatius in his epistle to the Smyrneans:

Wheresoever the bishop shall appear, there let the people also be; as where Jesus Christ is, there is the Catholic church.[37]

In this context, 'catholic' would have meant universal or orthodox, as opposed to factional or schismatical.

In the first two centuries of the Christian era, it was the local Roman officials who were largely responsible for the state persecution of Christians. In the second century, the emperors treated Christianity as a local problem to be dealt with by their subordinates. However, the number and severity of persecutions of Christians in various locations of the empire seemingly increased during the reign of Marcus Aurelius (161-180 AD). Sometimes, suspected Christians were hauled before the authorities and asked to offer incense to the emperor as a token of their worship. Of course, this was a blasphemy for Christians, and many refused to do so. Unfortunately, this often led to Christians being sentenced to death, since this was a grievous crime. As more and more Christians were being persecuted, a few brave voices spoke up in their defense, and even petitioned the emperor in writing. Although many of the apologetic defenses were eloquent, they had little overall effect.[38]

THIRD CENTURY PERSECUTION

IN the year 202 AD, the Roman emperor Septimius Severus enacted a law prohibiting the spread of Christianity and Judaism. This was the first universal decree forbidding conversion to Christianity. The tone was changed – from letting locals beat up Christians, to instigating across-the-board imperial persecution. In 238 AD, emperor Maximinus Thrax ('the Thracian') started a campaign to arrest and execute popes and bishops, hoping to eradicate the religion by killing the leaders. In 250 AD, the emperor Decius, wanting to restore the old Roman spirit and tradition, published an edict calling for a return to the pagan state religion. Local commissioners were appointed to enforce the ruling, and many did so with vigor. Anyone suspected of being a Christian was treated as a traitor and dealt with accordingly. The Decius persecution was the first of the two great systematic persecutions against Christians.

After the empire had suffered a number of military reverses during the first few years of the reign of emperor Valerian,[39] who had succeeded Decius, he issued an edict in 257 AD ordering the Christians to observe the ceremonies of the official Roman state religion. At the same time, he banned all activities in Christian subterranean burial places, which he then confiscated along with other Christian properties. Then in 258 AD, he issued another edict (the infamous Edict of 258), which was crueler and even more oppressive. This edict contained four commands regarding the treatment of Christians:

1) bishops, priests, and deacons were to be found and executed at once

2) confessing (to be a Christian) Roman senators, high officials, and military leaders were to be deprived of their position, honors, and possessions; and if after losing all this they continued to confess, then they were to be executed

3) Christian women were to be dispossessed of their property and banished (to a brothel, boarding house, or prison)

4) confessing members of the imperial household were to be deprived of their goods and sent in chains to their estates.[40]

Tough stuff, but in reality it was enforced only irregularly. Many bishops, priests, and deacons, however, quickly went into hiding in the countryside or the mountains.

In 286 AD, an entire Roman legion (called the Theban Legion) who had converted en-masse to Christianity, were martyred together. The army garrison was quartered in the city of Thebes in Egypt, until the emperor Maximian ordered them to march to Gaul, in Europe, to assist him in fighting against the rebels of Burgundy.[41] At Saint-Moritz, Switzerland (then called Agaunum),[42] orders were given to put to death a tenth of the men for mutiny and treason – since the legion had refused to give sacrifice to the Emperor.[43] This act was repeated twice before the entire legion was put to death. Legend has it that 6666 men were martyred, but modern-day scholars believe that the number is probably much lower.[44] Studious estimates range from 500 to 50 to as few as 5. But the account of 'The Martyrs of Agaunum' struck a resounding chord among early closet Christians – resonating with their desire to take the moral high-ground in their faith. Many pilgrimages from all over the empire were made to Saint-Maurice (renamed from Agaunum) to honor the saints. By name, 25 saints are associated with the Theban Legion, and two of those are women.

Within the imperial body-politic, the perceived problem of the Christians was diverting time, energy, and resources away from other more important state activities, such as quelling internal rebellions and repelling barbarian invaders crossing the borders. The Christians were willing to integrate into society, follow most Roman laws, and partake of most Roman customs. They just couldn't disavow their religion – it was simply too important to them. All they wanted was the freedom to practice the customs of their faith – even though those customs appeared odd in comparison with societal norms. And unfortunately for the Romans, they kept growing in number. Mass persecutions couldn't stop the expanding and spreading movement. They were no longer just a troublesome sub-cult of the Jews. They had become a dominant religious force in and of themselves. In some towns, the Christians outnumbered the pagans. And they were becoming more and more organized. Something had to be done.

EARLY FOURTH CENTURY PERSECUTION

IN 303 AD, the second great systematic persecution against Christians started under emperor Diocletian. Many provincial governors issued decrees that all inhabitants had to take part in sacrifices to the Roman gods, to help bring stability and prosperity to the empire. Christians who were denounced to the authorities were formally charged with insurrection if they would not renounce their religion and perform a sacrifice to the pagan gods. The city of Nicomedia,[45] capitol of the Roman province of Bithynia (today: northern Turkey along the Black Sea coast from Istanbul on eastward), was at the center of the great persecution of Christians which occurred from 301-304 AD under the eastern emperor Diocletian, the eastern junior-emperor Galerius, the western emperor Maximian, and the western junior-emperor Constantius I.[46] Nicomedia was Diocletian's chief place of residence and was half-Christian, the imperial palace itself being filled with Christians. On 23 February (the pagan festival of the Terminalia),[47] Diocletian ordered that the newly built main Christian church at Nicomedia be razed, its books and scriptures burned, and its precious stones seized. The next day he issued his 'First Edict Against the Christians', which ordered similar measures to be taken at churches across the Empire.

The destruction of the Christian church in Nicomedia incited panic in the city. At the end of the month, a fire destroyed part of Diocletian's palace, followed 16 days later by another fire. Although an investigation made into the cause of the fires resulted in no party being officially charged, Galerius placed the blame squarely on the Christians. He oversaw the execution of two palace eunuchs, who he claimed conspired with the Christians to start the fire. This was followed by six more executions through the end of April. Soon after, Galerius declared Nicomedia to be unsafe and ostentatiously departed the city for Rome – followed soon after by Diocletian. But the persecution only increased. Many massacres transpired throughout the Christian communities of Bithynia when altars were set up in the marketplaces, and transactions were not permitted until a token sacrifice to the Roman gods and to the divinity of the emperor, had been performed. Many people scattered to the countryside.

At the request of members of his congregation, Anthimus (or Anthony), the bishop of Nicomedia, took refuge in the small village of Omana, where he provided aid to survivors and sent letters exhorting the Christians to stand firm. When the soldiers of general Maximinus (who became eastern junior-emperor in 305 AD) were sent to find him, he welcomed them and fed them before revealing to them who he was. Amazed at his kindness, the soldiers promised that they would not tell Maximinus that they had found him. But Anthimus returned with them nevertheless, and converted and baptized them along the way.

A major calamity and persecution occurred when a main church that held numerous Christian worshippers was set fire to on Christmas Day. This event took place when the western emperor Maximian returned from victory over the Parthians in 304 AD. It occurred after the Christians had refused to sacrifice to idols during the Christmas Mass, when ordered to do so to thank the gods for the Roman victory. Maximian and his soldiers entered the church and told the Christians they could only escape punishment if they renounced Christ. The Christian priest Glycerius answered that the Christians would never "renounce their faith, even under the threat of torture". Maximian then ordered the church with everyone in it to be burned to the ground. Those who were not killed in the church fire were subsequently hunted down, captured, and tortured to death. Bishop Anthimus, who had escaped the burning of the church, was captured and beheaded. The overall number of martyrs was publicized as 20,000, but most modern scholars think that this is probably exaggerated.[48] In many cases, derision and ridicule accompanied their end. Some were covered with bodies of dead animals and left to be torn to death by wild dogs. And some were fastened on crosses, and when daylight faded, were torched with fire to serve as lamps by night.

CONVENTIONAL PERSECUTION HISTORY

Conventional history teaches that the early persecution of Christians can be broken down into three designated periods. The first period lasted from 64 to 112 AD (the reigns of emperor Nero through emperor Trajan). During this period, falsehoods spread throughout the populace about indecent orgies (baptismal rites), sacrifices (almsgiving), and cannibalism (blessed sacrament). People became so suspicious that they linked any calamity to the Christian presence. The local response was a round-up, followed by quick trial and sentence, in order to eliminate the presence. All of the Apostles were martyred except Saint John, known as the 'beloved disciple'. His persecutors tried to burn him alive in boiling oil, but he survived. So, he was exiled to the barren Greek island of Patmos, where he wrote the Book of Revelation. He died of old age about 100 AD after returning from exile to his home in Ephesus.[49]

The second period lasted from 112 to 186 AD (the reigns of emperor Trajan through emperor Commodus).[50] Most of the animosity toward Christians in this period was of the mob mentality. When a group of people became incensed over something, they took out their frustrations on the Christians – sometimes legally, and sometimes lawlessly using back-alley justice.

The third period was from 186 to 312 AD (the reigns of emperor Commodus through emperor Constantine).[51] This period witnessed the bloodiest of the persecutions. Under emperor Diocletian, the most pervasive and intense persecution took place – during the years 303 to 305 AD, entire families, groups, and congregations were tortured and put to death.

Finally, in 313 AD, co-emperors Licinius and Constantine issued the Edict of Milan,[52] proclaiming the common policy of full toleration for all religions and restitution of wrongs done to the Christians.[53] Christians could come out into the open for the first time. The third period of Roman persecution was over per the history books, but of course, persecutions continued on-and-off up until 380 AD, especially under the emperor Julian the Apostate (emperor 361-363 AD).[54] Julian was raised Christian but secretly abandoned Christianity in 351 AD after fraternizing with pagan philosophers. Christians were then forbidden to teach in the schools, certain bishops were exiled (including Athanasius of Alexandria), taxes were levied on Christian clergy, preference was given to pagans in appointments, etc. But most persecutions ended in 380 AD when emperor Theodosius declared Nicene Christianity to be the official religion of the empire.[55] At that point, the tables were turned and paganism was outlawed, and then even persecuted.

NOTES

---

1. Acts 8:3

2. There was an 'inner core' of 70 disciples (Luke 10:1-20) who maintained close affiliation with the Apostles, attending daily prayer meetings and services. It is believed that most, if not all of the 70, along with their families, fled Jerusalem at this time. They went to Egypt, North Africa, Mesopotamia, Assyria, Cyprus, Asia Minor, Greece, and even to Rome, probably to stay with relatives.

3. The good roads and transportation systems set in place by the Romans undoubtedly contributed to the rapid spread of the faith throughout the empire.

4. Acts 1:8

5. Simon Magus was even baptized (see Acts 8:13), but only in the Name of Jesus and not in the Name of the Holy Spirit.

6. In fact, Simon Magus became a real thorn in the side of Peter. He never forgave him for the public rebuke. Sometimes known as 'the father of Gnosticism', Simon traveled to Rome where he embarked on a career of ambitious huckstering and mongering. There, he performed such acclaimed magic acts that he became well known, was regarded as a god, and honored with a statue on an island in the river Tiber. All the while, he pretended that it was he who appeared among the Jews as the 'Son of Man', in Samaria as the 'Father', and among other nations as the 'Holy Spirit'. Many scholars conjecture that this is the reason why Peter traveled to Rome – Simon was a threat to the Christian ministry – he had to be stopped. In Rome, Peter confronted him on many occasions, and there are many apocryphal stories of what transpired ("The Acts of Peter", "The Acts of Peter and Paul", "The Pseudo-Clementine Recognitions and Homilies"). Simon eventually died (ignominiously, according to most accounts), but fantastic stories of Simon the Sorcerer persisted into the late Middle Ages.

7. For example, refer to the story about the riot of the silversmiths in Acts 19:23-40.

8. See Acts 9:2.

9. The actual word used in the edict was 'Chrestus', but this is considered just a linguistic or typographical error by historians.

10. Claudius was not prejudiced against the Jews. Near the same time as the Roman expulsion, he issued decrees giving the Jews in Alexandria, Egypt, more rights and freedoms.

11. Rome was the epicenter of all kinds of cult worship and associated decadence and debauchery in the civilized world. It was like a magnet for bizarre and unfamiliar 'foreign' thinking. Christians were just another one of many such groups that the ordinary citizen had to put up with. All the cults were persecuted to some extent, but the Christians were singled out because of what the gentry perceived to be excessively strange and unnatural behavior.

12. The fickle word of a snoop, meddler, gossiper, or busybody was often enough to warrant seizure and arrest.

13. The Jews of Asia (modern day Turkey) appear frequently in leading roles advocating the persecution of Christians. The persecution under Nero may have been due to their instigation.

14. The memorial (feast day) for the 'First Martyrs of the Church of Rome' is a replacement for the memorials of dozens of unfamiliar martyred individuals, most of whom have scant historical evidence.

15. Largely made up of wooden tenements, fire was a frequent occurrence in the city of Rome.

16. Cornelius Tacitus (trans. by J. Jackson), *The Annals of Imperial Rome and Agricola* (Book XV:44), [Cambridge: Harvard University Press, 1937]

17. The conversion of Paul (with name change from Saul to Paul) had occurred in 36-37 AD.

18. Unfortunately, nowhere in Scripture or in any other religious or historical writing, is her name revealed.

19. Reference: A.D. Clement, presbyter of Rome, in his signature work "Stromateus" in Eric Osborn, *Clement of Alexandria* [Cambridge: University Press, 2008].

20. It is entirely likely that Peter's wife contributed to the apostolic mission by sharing her own witness of who Jesus was and what he meant to her and to the world. It must have been a grand testimony! Surely, she knew Jesus personally. The story in Mark 1:29-31 implies that she prepared food and provided hospitality for Jesus in her own home (and probably not only on one occasion, as Jesus' Galilean ministry was centered in the area). She must have listened to Jesus' teaching and, without doubt, she was an intimate witness to his influence on her husband and his brother Andrew!

21. present-day Baalbek, Lebanon

22. There were already many Christians in Samaria – even a fledgling church – resulting from Jesus' interaction with the woman at the well (John 4:4-42), the miracle cure of the 10 lepers (Luke 17:11-19), and the preaching of Philip, Peter, and John after the resurrection of Christ (Acts 8:5-25).

23. Matthew 25:31-46

24. 'Ephigenia' is sometimes spelled as 'Iphigenia', and she is often incorrectly listed as 'Iphigenia of Abyssinia'. The story spread to African Ethiopia and she has a cult following there, but the region of Matthew's evangelism was Asian and not African.

25. Saint Matthew was spreading the Gospel to the region of 'Ethiopia' (a slang term for regions southwest of the Caspian Sea, probably near Edessa). He is said to be the Apostle of a Nation, as Bartholomew is for Armenia and Thomas is for Parthia and India. Matthew was the travelling partner of Thomas when they were sent out 'two-by-two' by Jesus (Mark 6:7). Some of Thomas' bones are preserved in Edessa, which is called 'Edessa of the Parthians'. Matthew preached the Gospel for 23 years, partly in Edessa, and partly in other regions of Parthia, while attaining many converts, founding innumerable churches, and setting up priests and bishops, in order to preserve the faith (as did all the Twelve who left Jerusalem).

26. After the emperor Augustus' death in 14 AD, he was declared divine, and shrines commemorating his divinity were built. All following emperors were also recognized as being divine, and great importance was attached to worshipping the emperor as a god. Failure to worship as required could have severe consequences. In addition, the Romans had many pagan gods, and not to give them homage meant invoking disapproval.

27. Pope Damasus I was able to convince the emperor Theodosius to recognize Christianity as the official state religion.

28. no doubt, from the custom of 'breaking bread' at the Lord's Supper – the partaking of the body and blood of Christ – the Holy Eucharist

29. Construction of the Colosseum began under the emperor Vespasian in 72 AD and was completed in 80 AD under his successor and heir Titus, with further modifications being made during the reign of Domitian in 81-96 AD (these three emperors are known as the Flavian dynasty).

30. The standard format for the Roman games was animal entertainment in the morning session, followed by the executions of criminals around midday, with the afternoon session reserved for gladiatorial combats and recreations of famous battles. The animal shows, which featured creatures from throughout the empire, included extravagant hunts and fights between different species. Animals also played a role in the execution of criminals, which were staged as recreations of myths and historical events.

31. Although the executions were seen as symbolizing Rome's power, the higher classes normally took advantage of this interval to leave the arena to dine. The executions were generally considered to be 'ho-hum' and beneath the level of haughty concern. Most returned in the afternoon to witness the grand combat spectacle.

32. These executions often took the form of the re-creation of some tragic scene from history or mythology with the criminal cast in the role of the victim.

33. Some Christians were executed as common criminals in the Colosseum – their crime being refusal to revere the Roman gods – but in actuality, most Christian martyrs were executed for their faith at the nearby Circus Maximus.

34. Saint Charbel was martyred in the Trajanic persecution of 107 AD.

35. The Christian church at Smyrna (in the Roman province of Asia; modern-day western Turkey), was one of the 'seven churches in the province of Asia' that is addressed in the beginning of the apocalyptic letter of Revelation (mentioned in Revelation 1:4). The seven churches were in the cities of Ephesus, Smyrna, Pergamum, Thyatira, Sardis, Philadelphia, and Laodicea (Revelation 1:11).

36. Polycarp suffered martyrdom in Smyrna along with 11 others from the church in Philadelphia. But he is the one who was remembered more than all the others – even by the pagans.

37. Reference: "The Epistle of Ignatius to the Smyrneans", in A. Roberts, J. Donaldson, and A. Cleveland Coxe, *Ante-Nicene Fathers*, *Vol. 1*, [Buffalo: Christian Literature Publishing Co., 1885].

38. The group of writers, starting in the 2nd century, who attempted to provide (at first in Greek and later in Latin) philosophical defenses of Christianity, and criticisms of Greco-Roman religious beliefs, are labeled as the 'early Christian apologists'.

Many of their writings were addressed to the Roman emperors Antoninus Pius and Marcus Aurelius. Most of the apologies assumed the form of briefs written to defend Christians against the accusations current in the society, namely that the religion was godless or that it was expressed in immoral carnal practices. They argued that, instead, their opponents were really the godless ones because they worshipped the gods of mythology. The most significant of the early apologists was Saint Justin Martyr, who wrote a treatise in 150 AD defending Christian morality, doctrine, and worship against pagan accusations. The seminal work seems to have had limited impact, however, as he was executed in Rome in 165 AD for offending the official state religion. The modern apologetic movement today (mostly concerned with defending against atheism and new-age religions) owes its start to these brave apologists.

39. Publius Licinius Valerianus

40. Among the most celebrated martyrs of this era are Pope Sixtus II (put to death with a number of deacons in the cemetery of Calixtus), and St. Cyprian of Carthage.

41. The Theban Legion was commanded in its march by Maurice (Mauritius), Candidus, and Exuperius (among others), all of whom are venerated as saints.

42. Saint Moritz is the modern name for the older town of Saint Maurice, which was renamed from Agaunum, after the legendary legionnaire Maurice of the Theban Legion had converted to Christianity and was martyred.

43. The purge of Christians in the military from 284 through 299 AD under emperor Diocletian, indicates that noncompliance with emperor worship was the common method for detecting Christian soldiers, and eventually executing them for mutiny.

44. The number 6666 itself, being the mark of the devil, as believed by many dogmatists, makes the tale highly suspect. It's as if the writer wanted the reader to have no doubt of its truth. Pragmatically, the number does not correspond to any military organizational unit.

45. Nicomedia was an ancient Greek city located in what is now Turkey. It was rebuilt from ruins by Nicomedes I of Bithynia in 264 BC under the name of Nicomedia, and has ever since been one of the most important cities in northwestern Asia Minor. Nicomedia was a metropolis and the capital of the Roman province of Bithynia under the Roman Empire. It is referenced repeatedly in Pliny the Younger's Letters to Trajan during his tenure as governor of Bithynia. In his letters, Pliny mentions several public buildings of the city such as a senate-house, an aqueduct, a forum, and the temple of Cybele – and speaks of a great fire, during which the place suffered much.

The emperor Diocletian made it the capital city of the Eastern Roman Empire in 286 AD when he introduced the Tetrarchy system of rule. Nicomedia remained as the eastern (and most senior) capital of the Roman Empire until co-emperor Licinius was defeated by Constantine the Great at the Battle of Chrysopolis in 324 AD, and ended the Tetrarchy. Constantine mainly resided in Nicomedia as his interim capital city for the next six years, until in 330 AD when he declared the nearby Byzantium, which was renamed Constantinople (modern-day Istanbul), to be the new capital. Constantine died in a royal villa in the vicinity of Nicomedia in 337 AD. Owing to its position at the convergence of the Asiatic roads leading to the new capital, Nicomedia retained its importance even after the founding of Constantinople.

46. In the Tetrarchy, the emperor was called 'Augustus' and the junior-emperor was called 'Caesar'. There was an emperor and junior-emperor in both the east and the west. In this book, these titles are generally not capitalized, although in period works they usually would be.

47. The Terminalia holiday was named after the Roman pagan god Terminus – the god of boundary stones and property lines.

48. Today, the martyrs of Nicomedia continue to be memorialized with feast days. In the Roman Catholic Church, there are separate entries for different groups of martyrs from Nicomedia. The martyrdom of bishop Anthimus (or Anthony), the priest Glycerius, and the victims of the church fire (and subsequent round-up) are commemorated on April 24. The aggregate martyrdom of Christians in the communities of Bithynia near Nicomedia, separate from the event of the church fire, is commemorated on June 23. In the Eastern Orthodox and Byzantine Catholic churches, the victims of the church fire are commemorated on 28 December.

49. Tradition holds that John lived until the reign of Trajan (98–117 AD).

50. Commodus was the emperor alluded to in the blockbuster movie *Gladiator* [Universal Pictures, 2000].

51. There is some overlap between imperial reigns and these arbitrary designated periods. Trajan was emperor from 98 to 117 AD, overlapping the first and second periods. Commodus was emperor from 180 to 192 AD, overlapping the second and third periods, and Constantine the Great was emperor from 306 to 337 AD [actually co-emperor from 306 to 324].

52. The agreements were made in Milan, although the Edict was issued in Nicomedia.

53. Constantine himself went further, making lavish donations to the churches and granting immunities to the clergy.

54. On his deathbed, it is rumored that Julian muttered, "You have conquered, Galilean." (meaning that the god of the new religion of Jesus of Galilee had overcome the gods of the ancient religion of the Greeks and Romans).

55. There were competing doctrines in Christian theology at the time. At the ecumenical Council of Nicaea (at modern Iznik, Turkey) in 325 AD (called by Constantine the Great), the doctrine of Arianism (the belief that Jesus was not God, but a created creature with a beginning) was rejected and a creed was issued (the Nicene Creed) to safeguard orthodox belief – that the Son is of 'one substance with the Father' (He is completely divine). Therefore, the orthodox doctrine was dubbed Nicene Christianity.

41

3 THE PERSECUTED

Who, Why, and How?

THE MARTYRS

To their fellow believers, the martyrs came to be viewed as victors over evil and death, and not just as victims of Roman oppression – they were harbingers of hope, ordained by none other than Almighty God. In the bodies of the martyrs, weakness became strength, shame became honor, and earthly death became eternal life.

As the stories of martyrs were recorded and spread from community to community, they fueled the growth of the Christian church. Through the telling and re-telling of their stories, Christians constructed a group identity based on suffering as empowerment, and death as victory. The crucifixion, death, and resurrection of Jesus, the incarnate Christ, served as the quintessential example of such victorious suffering. Jesus lived in the body, taught in the body, suffered in the body, and died in the body. For the early Christians, it was this very human body that was understood to be the conduit between God and human beings. It was no accident that the bodies of the martyrs became the focus of activity in the unfolding drama of the spread of Christianity – a drama that transformed the helplessness of the individual, no matter the rank, into his authority and control of self-determination

– and transformed the meekness of the faith into the dominant religion of the empire. In the stead of Christ, the suffering martyr served as mediator between God and the world. In the body of the martyr, death was unmasked as the gateway to eternal life. As Christ's death and resurrection were understood to redeem the world, so too the death of the Christian martyr continued that work of redemption on behalf of Christ. They made the possibility of victory through resurrection, for all who believed, very real. The martyr bore witness to the solidarity between suffering humanity and the trinitarian God, who became incarnate in the life of Jesus Christ. And this witness was effectual regardless of gender.

Martyrs were considered holy persons – consequently, they were highly honored. Although not always possible, noble Christians sought to gather their remains after death, which led to the custom of the veneration of relics; as well as the construction of many shrines, memorials, and holy places organized around the bodies (or relics) of the saints, both women and men.

EARLY PERSECUTION OF WOMEN

FIRST century historical records are very sketchy. It's almost impossible to separate conjecture and hype from fact and truth. There are surviving writings, secular and religious, that mention this or that, him or her, but it's difficult to validate anything against official records. However, it is no exaggeration to say that although not as numerous as men, Christian women also suffered dearly for their faith.

Julia Livia

Although not officially documented and independently verified, it is possible that the actual first woman to be mortally persecuted as a Christian for her faith was Julia

Caesaris Drusus, or commonly known as Julia Livia, daughter of Drusus Julius Caesar and Lavilla Claudius Caesar, granddaughter of the emperor Tiberius, first cousin of the emperor Caligula, and niece of the emperor Claudius. This was more than just an embarrassment with a slap on the wrist – she was involved in a web of political intrigue within the Roman nobility.

In 43 AD, empress Valeria Messalina, an agent of the wife of emperor Claudius, falsely charged Julia with incest (which was illegal) and immorality. Messalina considered Julia and her son to be a threat to the throne, but the trumped-up charges grew out of the supposition that she was a 'Christian' and had forsaken the Roman gods and morals (which they presumed most Christians did). Without securing any defense for his niece, Claudius had her executed 'by the sword'. Knowing this, her distant relative Pomponia Graecina remained in mourning for 40 years in subtle defiance of the emperor, yet was unpunished.

Thecla

A follower of Paul, and a young woman consecrated to Christ, Thecla was twice sentenced to death for failing to respect the Roman social customs, which she believed were anathema to her belief in the Christian religion. And twice her execution attempts failed. She had heard the sermons of Saint Paul in her hometown in 47-48 AD,[1] become an ardent disciple, and left her mother and fiancé to follow Paul. When thrown into the gladiatorial arena, neither wild beasts, burning at the stake, nor dragging by bulls could defeat her or destroy her spirit. Facing death before baptism, at the last moment she threw herself into a large vat of water filled with dangerous leopard seals, and baptized herself – and again she was not harmed. Thinking she was a goddess, the governor released her, whereupon she met up with Paul, and followed him on part of his First Missionary Voyage.

Eventually, she was commissioned by Paul to go out and preach the gospel – the first female missionary and evangelist. Although she lived as an ascetic to an old age, she is considered a martyr because serious execution attempts were made, and she was willing to lay down her life for the faith. The story is disputed by some historians, but there is convincing archeological evidence in southeastern Turkey for the existence of an ascetic named Thecla.[2]

Damaris

A biblical figure who became the first converted Christian in Athens was a woman named Damaris.[3] She was one of those present when Paul preached there in front of the Athenian Areopagus in 55 AD.[4] Standing with Dionysius the Areopagite,[5] she embraced the Christian faith following Paul's speech, along with unnamed others.

Since women were usually not present in these meetings, Damaris has traditionally been assumed to have been a courtesan (an educated woman who provided companionship and intellectual stimulation to public figures), a high-status prostitute, a follower of the Stoics (who welcomed women among their ranks), or a foreigner visiting Athens. She may have been the wife of Dionysius, but most scholars doubt that. There are conflicting unreliable accounts on this, but it is possible that together with two other disciples of Dionysius, they all became martyrs. Even if true, the exact date and place of martyrdom are unknown (but was probably prior to 96 AD).

Pomponia Graecina

In secular historical records, the very first woman to be persecuted as a Christian for her faith occurred about 57 AD.[6] Her name was Pomponia Graecina, and she was a woman of noble rank. She was accused of 'foreign superstition' (an aphorism for being a Christian) by her husband Aulus Plautius and handed over to him for trial,[7] where he was also to be the judge. She was tried according to Roman custom for her 'abandonment of the national worship' in the presence of her kindred. Legally, she was acquitted, but socially she was ostracized, living in great sorrow and 'wearing no habit but that of mourning' until her death in 83 AD.[8] It is thought that Pomponia was one of the 'saints' that were in Caesar's household, mentioned by Paul in Philippians 4:22.[9]

Claudia Rufina

Another possible 'saint' of Caesar's household was Claudia Rufina, wife of the Roman senator Aulus Pudens, and daughter of a British king who had come to Rome. It is also thought that she was the mother of Linus, Peter's successor as Bishop of Rome.[10] In 2 Timothy 4:21, Paul conveys his greetings to Timothy by saying, "Eubulus sends greetings to you, as do Pudens and Linus and Claudia and all the brothers and sisters." Celebrated for her admirable beauty and learning, Claudia sent Paul's writings, which she called 'spiritual manna', to her friends in Briton (since she grew up there), to 'feed their souls with the bread of life'.[11]

Helena

According to oral tradition, at some time between 62 and 68 AD, the two children of Alphaeus (one of the 70 disciples of Jesus,[12] who worked closely with the other apostles in spreading the Gospel), Abercius and Helena, were martyred for confessing their faith in Christ. Alphaeus himself, had been bound to a cross and shot through with arrows, dying as a martyr. The supposition is that the son and daughter were martyred as adults shortly after their father. Abercius was tied naked to a beehive and died from the bees' stings. Helena was pelted with stones until she was dead. She is generally recognized as the first named female martyr saint.

Basilissa and Anastasia

Among the first converts to Christianity who were martyred in the 1st century were the Roman matrons Basilissa and Anastasia. Disciples of high rank and great wealth, they were probably baptized by the apostle Peter or Paul. After the martyrdom of the two apostles, it is thought that they were responsible for giving them 'honorable Christian burials'.[13] The burials likely exposed Basilissa and Anastasia to further persecution, and they were eventually arrested for collecting the relics, and burying the bodies of other martyred Christians. They refused to renounce their Christian faith, and after being tortured mercilessly (including having their tongues torn out, their skins pierced with sharp hooks, bodies burned with fire, and their breasts and feet cut off), they were beheaded with swords by order of Nero in 68 AD.[14]

Petronilla and Felicula

In unofficial religious writings, there is the fabled story of Petronilla, who may have been a blood daughter, a servant, or a convert (a 'spiritual daughter', or a follower) of Saint Peter, the Apostle. It is said that Peter cured her of palsy. She was so beautiful that when a pagan Roman official, named Flaccus, aggressively wished to marry her, but Petronilla refused the offer, she had to be locked up in a tower for protection against the angry rejected suitor. This led Petronilla to go on a hunger strike, from which she never fully recovered and eventually died.

Her actual name may have been Aurelia Petronilla. It's very possible that she was a relative of a high-ranking Christian family who were related to a royal senatorial family (the Flavius). This could explain why she was buried in the catacomb of Flavia Domatilla, niece to one of the consuls of Rome. Like Flavia, Petronilla may have suffered during the persecution of emperor Domitian (81-96 AD).

Petronilla had a foster sister named Felicula who also became a Christian. She was arrested and put in prison for creating a disturbance when she sided with her sister in protesting against the unwanted harassment by the rejected pagan suitor. After Petronilla's death, Felicula became sick from malnourishment in prison, being given very little food and water. With no advocate to help her, no money, and very little strength, she was despised by the prison officials and treated as a waif. To rid themselves of the problem, she was eventually thrown into a sewer, where she died in 90 AD. Felicula is recognized as one of the first virgin martyrs.

Flavia Domatilla

As previously mentioned, a high-ranking woman who suffered for her faith was Flavia Domatilla. Granddaughter of emperor Vespasian and wife of consul Titus Flavius Clemens,[15] she was charged with professing Christ during the period of targeted persecutions around 96 AD, and punished by banishment to the island of Pontia,[16] along with many others. The official charge was atheism (the charge on which many people who drifted into Jewish and Christian ways were condemned). This was during the same round of persecutions when the Apostle John was exiled to the Greek island of Patmos.[17]

PERSECUTION OF UNMARRIED WOMEN

IN a culture where one's possibilities in life were largely predetermined by class, wealth, and gender, asceticism could be seen as a discipline that allowed for some form of individual control. Even if people could not change the political, social, or economic structures of the world, they could change their behavior. Especially for women, a life of celibacy delivered them from some of the undesirable constraints normally imposed upon them. A life of virginity also meant that the risks of childbirth were avoided. Ancient women suffered from complications at childbirth far more often than is the case for women in industrialized countries today. Lastly, celibate women had opportunities for meaningful work and service usually not available to married women.

But in the Roman world, 'good girls' became mothers. Becoming a mother, bearing children that survived (ideally sons) for her husband and for the stability of the household, was essential to being a 'good wife'. Rejecting the 'blessedness' of motherhood for future rewards in a foreign kingdom was threatening to an empire that prided itself on establishing peace for the whole world (the 'Pax Romana'). It was seen as subversive. The Romans didn't take kindly to subversives or spies working for a foreign land that could possibly be an enemy waiting to pounce. In any case, for the empire to survive and thrive, it needed children.

The 15 years leading up to 313 AD witnessed the death and martyrdom of many young unmarried girls (virgins); those who had consecrated themselves as a bride of Christ rather than be subjected to undesirable marriage arrangements, which was common at the time.[18] Paul's teaching on celibacy made a great deal of sense to many people very quickly in the early church – it especially struck a chord with young women. His basic message was that people should remain pure in anticipation of the resurrection – dedicated celibacy and virginity anticipate the life of glory after the resurrection, when marriage will no longer exist – which is coming soon – so it would be well to get ready for it. Of course, the definition of 'purity' is at the core of the message, and many took the message in its strictest sense. The end result was that young women were renouncing potential husbands and young men were renouncing potential wives. A woman who did this surely defied the societal expectations of the time – but was often extremely popular. She was a rebel with a cause.

The apostle Paul was a hard-working, much traveled single guy, who maintained that he wouldn't have gotten nearly as much accomplished if he had had a family to tie him down. His simple message was 'in practice, celibacy beats marriage'.[19] Many young girls took this to heart and saw it as a way out of an undesirable arranged marriage. Better to remain single and pure in the eyes of God – helping them to obtain the rewards of salvation, resurrection, and eternal life – than to be unhappily married to a pagan and burdened with earthly responsibilities, thereby hindering their chances for salvation. An oft-used excuse was that they were already married to Christ.

There are many examples of young women who saw Christ as their spouse and thus refused betrothals. This often brought them into conflict with either their fathers or their betrothed, who out of spite often handed them over to the local Roman authorities for punishment. In some cases, the issue was civil, if the woman's religious convictions were not brought to notice – she just wanted out of the marriage arrangement. In those cases, the punishment could be banishment to a brothel, if she didn't relent. However, when the case became religious oriented – she refused to worship the emperor or the gods – there were legal and criminal ramifications – and the punishment would likely be torture, and death in the end extreme. There were few sanctuaries for runaway girls seeking escape from matrimony – living hermit-like in the woods or desert with a group community (if one could be found) or living secretly underground in the protection of fellow believers, were pretty much the only options. And it was dangerous – there were pursuers who wanted revenge or a bounty. Martyrdom became the ultimate escape to freedom.

For the record, in this book, and in the records of the early Christian church, the category ascribed to young unmarried women is 'virgin'. It really means a young woman of child-bearing age who has renounced matrimony and sexual relations. It's just a simple categorization criterion (one word instead of 13), since the quality is fairly easy to identify. Girls under 12 were generally not counted – they are considered children. And never-married women over 30 were generally ignored. Of course, the actual sexual maturity of any one individual is not really relevant for categorization purposes, and is probably lost (or never documented) in the annals of historical records anyhow. It should be noted that young unmarried men are not separated out in such a manner.

MARTYRDOM AND SAINTHOOD OF WOMEN

IN the forthcoming years of increasing persecution, many women became martyrs, and many martyrs became saints. In antiquity, the human body was understood on a hierarchical continuum. The male sex represented the highest level, while the female sex represented the secondary level. Furthermore, personal virtues were associated with biological sex. The higher virtues (justice, self-control, courage) were considered to be male virtues, while the lesser virtues (gentleness, modesty, chastity) were understood as female. The female martyr faced the challenge of being and remaining female, even as she moved up the hierarchical continuum of virtue, toward greater and greater maleness, and ultimately to Christ.

A woman's exhibition of manly virtues proved her superiority to the persecutors. At the same time, her show of feminine virtues reinforced her accepted role in society.

The strength of the martyr, like that of Christ, was revealed in his or her weakness. This is portrayed most vividly in the body of the feeble vulnerable woman who died in the process of mimicking Christ, and professing the faith – and there were many such women. Whether female or male, the martyrs were understood as participants in the drama of redemption. The body of the martyr, no matter how low in social status, served as the vessel through which that martyr became one with Christ. Hence, even one so low on the spectrum as an illiterate, unrefined, female slave, could take a noble part in the salvation of humankind. For believers, such a transformation was powerful. It illustrated that anyone, even the lowest of the low, who suffered for the glory of Christ, would have fellowship forever with God in heaven. The possibility and hope for a new life, one free of inequity, injustice, and pain, was made available to all. Throughout history, the stories of the Christian martyrs have served as beacons of such hope.

In the following chapter are the stories of some of the most well-known heroes – unmarried women, slaves, and unmarried slaves. The appendices provide a more comprehensive list of heroes.

Sainthood

Many women became saints for various virtuous reasons in addition to martyrdom. In general, women that have been canonized as saints fall into one of six categories:[20]

Biblical Figures

Martyrs

Virgin Martyrs (and child martyrs)

Founders or Benefactors

Ascetics and Exceptionally Pious Individuals [21]
Visionaries/Legends [22]

In Appendix I is a list of all the heroic women mentioned in this book – those most commonly recognized by the Christian religious traditions as saints or holy martyrs. This is not the ultimate comprehensive definitive listing, but it does give a sharp insight into the history and culture of the time period between 33 AD (or the resurrection of Jesus Christ) and 313 AD (the abolishment of official Christian persecution by the Roman Empire). Crude estimates can be obtained for numbers of individuals involved, but an accurate tally is impossible because of the large uncertainty in the historical accounts (especially regarding large groups of individuals in a common scenario).

It should be noted that many martyrs did not become saints for any number of reasons. Often, they were just one member of a large group, or were of such low status that names were not considered important. Where these martyrs are vaguely mentioned in the few historical records that exist, they have been included in this book, since their lives are no less important than the lives of distinguished individuals.

The stories of the saints come from a variety of sources. Some saints lived long before accurate historical records were kept, and some are legendary with no way to obtain independent verification. Others are known for their writings or their deeds, and others are only remembered because someone else knew them and recorded the events in their lives. As with life in general, there are numerous sides to every story and discrepancies in every tale. Of course, that is the case with the stories in this book. While there is no intent to write blatant fiction here, the ultimate level of pure truth in each story is known only to God. To be sure, all the saints and martyrs have contributed to the quest of praising and realizing the kingdom of God, both on earth and in heaven. In so doing, they have enriched the spiritual sense and understanding of all who have followed. Their names, lives, and stories must not be forgotten.

THE SLAVES

THE torturing of slaves to obtain trial evidence against their masters would undoubtedly scandalize modern sensibilities. But in Roman society, it was a logical consequence of the position of slaves in the societal hierarchy. As witnesses to the deeds and actions of citizens, slaves knew everything that went on in Rome, but at the same time were totally dependent on their masters and would only speak at their command. Interrogating slaves about their masters was like asking the masters to incriminate themselves. However, physical torture could free slaves from submission to their masters by enslaving them to their own bodies. Then they would speak not to obey their master but to obey the dictates of pain. It was thought that slaves had no disposition, were devoid of moral autonomy, and if they were no longer guided by their masters' will, then they would be led by sensuality and natural instincts/impulses. And as everyone in Rome knew perfectly well, people instinctively sought to escape pain.[23]

However, it should be noted that there were plenty of instances in which the tortured slaves did not give testimony (true or false) against their masters merely to save their own skins.[24] In the end, the Roman courts understood that torture was not always effective as a means of learning the truth of a case: "It is stated in our constitutions that trust should not always be given to torture, but torture should not always be rejected. Torture is a weak and dangerous thing that may fail the truth. Many people have the patience and endurance to be contemptuous of torture. The truth can never be extracted from them. Others have so little patience that they would tell any kind of lie rather than suffer torture." [25]

Many Christians living in the first three centuries expected that the world would end soon – within their own life-time or the life-time of their children. Consequently, they were mostly concerned with the urgent matter of salvation – repentance from former sins, betterment of their behavior, and spreading of the Good News to everyone who was open to listening. They weren't much concerned with changing the world – it was beyond their aspirations and imagination. Besides, questioning a universally accepted institution, such as slavery, could be considered subversive – and that was the last thing they wanted, given society's already perceived notions and concerns about them.

Slaves make their appearance in the Gospels as a matter of course. They serve their masters and perform the tasks expected of them without provoking any protests from Jesus or his disciples. The first missionaries of the Gospel, men of Jewish origin, came from a country where slavery existed. But it existed in a form very different from the Roman form. The Mosaic Law was merciful to the slave,[26] and carefully secured a fair wage for the laborer.[27] In Jewish society, the slave was not an object of contempt, because labor was not a thing to be despised as it was elsewhere. No Jew thought it beneath him to ply a manual trade.[28] The Apostles and disciples brought these ideas and habits of life with them – the Good News – into the new society ('The Way') which so rapidly grew up as the effect of their preaching. As this society included, from the first, faithful of all conditions – rich and poor, slaves and freemen – the Apostles simply pronounced these beliefs when confronted with the social inequalities that plagued the Roman world.

All of you who have been baptized into Christ have clothed yourselves with him. There does not exist among you Jew or Greek, slave or freeman, male or female. All are one in Christ Jesus. It was in one Spirit that all of us, whether Jew or Greek, slave or free, were baptized into one body. [29]

In the New Testament, slaves are admonished to obey their masters, not only those who were kind and reasonable but also those who were harsh.[30] By showing respect and honor for their masters, slaves could ensure that the name of God and the moral teaching of the faith would not be brought into disrepute.[31] Indeed, serving their masters sincerely was their role and obligation. Not only were they to obey when being watched, but they were to always do the will of God from their hearts.[32] It was thus expected that complete fidelity and obedience on their part, would add credit to Christian doctrine and teaching.[33]

While in prison, Paul received at some point, the services of a runaway slave named Onesimus. Although recognizing his usefulness to himself, Paul felt obliged to send him back to his lawful Christian owner, as was socially proper at the time. But since the slave had been earnestly converted to the new faith, Paul pleaded that he be forgiven for his unacceptable past behavior and not be punished severely (as was common in such cases). But he was nevertheless meant to remain a slave unless Philemon felt stirred to free him,[34] which is probably what happened since he is mentioned again in Colossians 4:9. In other words, everyone should remain in whatever social status he found himself when he was called to the faith. "

"Brothers, each of you should continue before God in the condition of life that was his when he was called."[35] A revolution against slavery was not on Paul's agenda (social revolution was not in the Christian storybook). The thinking at the time was that 'masters should remain masters, while slaves should remain slaves'.[36]

Early Christian doctrine accepted society as it is. Directly changing the ills of society was not its policy. Nevertheless, society would be transformed indirectly through the reaching and influence of individual souls. What Christianity demanded from masters and from slaves, was to live in harmony as neighbors – giving and receiving – commanding and obeying – with equity, remembering that God is the master of all.[37]

PERSECUTION OF SLAVES

Agricultural slaves were numerous in the Roman world. Most of them worked on large farms of wealthy landowners and were often kept in dirty barracks. They were supervised by stewards, who were either slaves themselves, or free-men enjoying the trust of their masters. Their living conditions were tough, and the treatment they received was often cruel. Such slaves normally participated in the common pagan feasts. But they were not allowed to make their own religious choice. And there were no significant attempts by Christian missionaries to convert them.

Many slaves, both male and female, were often sexually exploited. When they were confined to brothels, their conditions of living could be very unhealthy and unpleasant. However, some female slaves became mistresses and concubines of wealthy men, princes, and even emperors. In such cases, they could live in luxury and were even able to exercise some power.

The bulk of Jesus' followers were originally peasants. On a normal working day, they were expected to be laboring as fieldworkers or fishermen, or grinding at the mill.[38] Many owned one or more slaves who assisted them in their workplace and household labors. Ploughing fields and tending sheep were clearly thought to be typical tasks of slaves.[39]

However, as soon as the Jesus movement began to spread beyond Palestine, it underwent a fundamental shift. While Jesus preached almost exclusively in rural areas, after Pentecost, most Christian missionaries, such as Paul and Barnabas, were visiting primarily the important urban towns of the empire. The originally rural movement was quickly transformed into an urban movement, and new converts were drawn from all social strata of the urban population. In addition, the ancient scorn of labor was absent among the believers in the new Christian religion. Converts to the new religion knew that Jesus had been a carpenter, Peter had been a fisherman, and Paul had been a tentmaker. At a time when those who performed manual labor were considered 'the dregs of the city' by the aristocracy, this new mindset was very appealing – and this included the great mass of workers and slaves. A new sentiment was introduced into the Roman world – Christians did not make a spectacle of their laziness or leisurely lounging – they labored in an occupation.

Gradually, some slaves began to join Christian communities. In general, they belonged to one of two privileged groups: the tradesman/artisan household/urban worker (with maybe a small plot of arable land) – such as Aquila and Priscilla, who were tentmakers,[40] and Lydia of Thyatira, who was a dealer in purple cloth[41] – OR – the regal/imperial household (the so-called 'family of Caesar') – such as those mentioned by Paul in his letter to the Philippians,[42] and the household in which lived Callistus (or Callixtus), the slave of a Christian master, who himself was a free-man of the emperor Commodus.[43] In fact, many of the people who Saint Paul salutes at the end of his Letter to the

Romans are actually servants or slaves in imperial households. Those "who belong to the family of Aristobulus" and those "who belong to the family of Narcissus" include the Christian slaves of those two imperial households that were contemporaries of the emperor Nero.[44]

In general, the pagan religion of the Romans excluded slaves from its functions. But the new religion of Christianity proclaimed religious equality for all – in ancient times, a novelty. The Church made no account of the social condition or sex of the faithful. Slave and master, bond and free, male and female, all received the same sacraments. According to Paul: "All are one in Christ Jesus."[45] And before long, clerics and church officials who were once slaves became numerous – even the very Chair of Saint Peter was occupied by men who had once been slaves.[46] In the Christian cemeteries there is no difference between the tombs of slaves and those of the free, whereas pagan tombs almost always indicated the servile condition of the deceased. Slaves who died as martyrs were often honored in prodigious manner. For example, the ashes of two slaves, Protus and Hyacinthus, who had been burned alive during the persecutions of emperor Valerian in 253-260 AD, were found to have been wrapped in a winding-sheet of gold tissue. Martyrdom eloquently manifested the religious equality of the slave.

To a large extent, the fate of slaves depended upon the wealth and power of their masters. Most owners didn't really care if their slaves had a religion, as long as they did their work properly. Besides, any religion of the slaves would just be uncivilized mumbo-jumbo anyhow, so they thought. But problems inevitably arose when slaves expressed the desire to become Christians. Permission by the master was required before a slave could request membership in another religion, especially since Christianity was a subversive cult. Not surprisingly, there was often tension between slaves desiring conversion to Christianity and pagan masters. Many rejections were followed by further master/slave distancing, retribution, and punishment (often physically harsh).

There was also frequent tension within Christian households. Many slaves who had been allowed by their Christian masters to join the new faith thought that this would lead to a relaxation of their earthly duties. But rarely was this the viewpoint of the master. An explicit countermanding reply to arguments that would give priority to the religious duties of slaves is given in the Book of Timothy.[47] However, it should be noted that some newly converted Christians freed all of their slaves within their lifetimes, effectively depriving themselves of a considerable part of their estate. There are no records of pagans doing this.[48]

Some Christian slaves went even further and expected that they should be emancipated simply because they had become Christians. Slaves in the Roman world could usually buy their freedom with enough money. Of course, very few slaves had this wherewithal, even if they had saved most of their lives. So, many turned to the Christian church communities for the requisite funds. This, in turn, led to further tensions because of all the competing elements desiring allocation of limited church resources.

Taking the desire for freedom to the extreme, some Christian slaves willfully chose to become martyrs. By becoming a Christian, the slave felt that he had no further obligations to his human master when it came to choosing between his earthly and his religious duties. And knowing that this would not be tolerated by the master or the civil authorities, he was actually envisaging freedom through an honorable death.

Notable Individuals

In the mid-second-century (~165 AD), a Christian slave of the emperor and a student of Saint Justin the Philosopher, named Evelpistos, was scourged for not obeying his master. At his interrogation, he replied to the prefect who was acting as judge,

Once Caesar's slave, I am now a slave of Christ, winning freedom by his favor.[49]

Needless to say, this didn't go over well – he was beheaded the following day (along with Justin and 5 others who refused to sacrifice to the gods and obey the imperial ordinances).

In the early fourth century, the famous Christian teacher Pamphilus was accompanied to his martyrdom by his slave Porphyry. Just 18 years old, Porphyry died after a long anguish, having been given, like many other martyrs, the opportunity to save himself.[50]

Slaves who chose to suffer, not at the hands of their masters but at the hands of persecutors, and who sought to serve God directly through their death, were treated with dignity and respect by the Fathers of the early church. They found a way of dying that gave better meaning to their servile mode of living. They aspired to liberation through what they understood of salvation and resurrection.

MARTYRDOM OF WOMEN SLAVES

Redemption for humanity through the suffering, death, and resurrection of Jesus Christ is intricately woven into the fabric of Christianity. The being who suffered and died on the cross is a personal, relational god – a Trinitarian God – who became incarnate and lived and died in solidarity with suffering humanity. The martyr bears self-witness to the solidarity between suffering humanity and God. He/she takes upon him/her self the features of Christ's suffering – like an imitation of Jesus. This witness is independent of gender. Whether male or female, the martyrs were understood to be participants in the drama of suffering and redemption. Even one at the very bottom of the social totem-pole was viewed as being a champion of the faith, and a true witness for Christ.[51]

For believers in the faith, such an image and representation were very powerful. It illustrated that everyone (even someone at the very bottom of the social strata – a slave and a woman) who suffers for the glory of Christ, has eternal fellowship with the living God. In that possibility, hope for a new life, one free of inequity and injustice, was made available to all.

The slave-girl martyr was probably equally motivated by faith and freedom. Salvation and liberty provided her with reasons to escape from the dreadfulness of everyday life. The slave-girl died for faith and freedom, equally threatened. Such a sensibility is found in the accounts of the martyrdoms of the slaves Zoe, Ariadne, Felicitas, Mary, Maxima, and others.

The Deaconesses of Bithynia – 112 AD

In the Roman province of Bithynia (modern day Turkey's northern Black Sea coast), two young maidservants were tortured, and probably killed by the provincial Roman governor Gaius Plinius Luci, known to history as 'Pliny the Younger'.[52] He had encountered a troublesome religious sect in the province and he wanted advice on how to deal with them – and so he wrote a letter to the emperor Trajan in Rome, inquiring as such. What he had learned about Christian beliefs and practices had been acquired from those Christians who apostatized – those who had first confessed their faith, but then denied their faith when confronted with the threat of execution. What he thought he had determined was this:

They met regularly before dawn on a fixed day to chant verses alternatively among themselves in honor of Christ, as if he was a god. They also bound themselves by oath to abstain from theft, robbery, and adultery, and to commit no breach of trust. After this ceremony, it was their custom to disperse and reassemble later to share ordinary everyday food and drink.

This revealing was so pathetically innocent that Pliny was suspicious of it. He needed to get at the truth of what was going on. One way to do that was to extract it from two slave women who were officials in the movement, called deaconesses.[53] In an infamous letter to Trajan, Pliny wrote, "I thought it the more necessary, therefore, to find out what truth there was in this [the accusation against Christians] by applying torture to two maidservants who were called 'ministers' [an obvious leadership role]. But I found nothing but a depraved and extravagant superstition"[54]

These deaconesses, or female ministers, were very probably slaves since they were called 'maidservants'. Yet they were recognized publicly as Christian 'ministers'. Their witness for Christ must have been outspoken, because they were arrested and endured great suffering and extensive torture, in an effort to get them to incriminate the rest of the church. But they did not recant their testimony to Christ.[55] These noble slave-girls, names unknown, became early martyrs to the cause of Christ.

The Martyrs of Pamphylia - between 127 and 138 AD

A family of Christian slaves in Attalia, Pamphylia,[56] were martyred under the persecution of emperor Hadrian, because their master had commanded them to participate in pagan rituals, but they all refused. In retaliation, they were burned to death. Zoe was the wife of Exuperius (sometimes called Hesperus), and they had two sons, Cyriacus and Theodulus. They were owned by a rich devout worshipper of the ancient pagan Roman gods, named Catullus. Zoe's job was to tend the house dogs and prevent them from biting visitors. She rarely saw her husband as he worked in the fields far from the house. Zoe was stationed near a roadway, and she freely gave of her own meagre rations to those even poorer than herself who passed by.

On the birthday of Catullus' son, a feast was prepared at the house in honor of the pagan goddess Fortuna. Food was sent to the slaves from the master's table, and this included meat and wine that had been sacrificed to idols. The slave family refused to participate and would not eat the food, Zoe being outspoken in the defense of her religion, which forbid such practice. Zoe poured the wine on the ground and threw the meat to the dogs.

When Catullus learned of this, he became incensed and forced the family to submit to torture, hoping to gain obedience. He gave orders to torture the young boys Cyriacus and Theodulus. The brothers were then stripped, suspended from a tree, and raked with hot iron implements before the eyes of their parents, who counselled their children to persevere to the end.

After this, Zoe and Exuperius were subjected to the most terrible tortures. But the family would not relent. Finally, the pagans threw all four family members into a red-hot furnace, where they surrendered their souls to the Lord. As the bodies were burning, it is said that angelic singing could be heard glorifying and praising the Lord.

The Passion of Perpetua and Felicitas – 203 AD

In 203 AD, a group of Christian believers and catechumens were tried, condemned, tortured, and executed, including two slaves, Revocatus and Felicitas. Revocatus and two other prisoners had been scourged before they were thrown to the beasts. It is said that they all rejoiced at having obtained a share in the Lord's sufferings. Being pregnant in her eighth month, Felicitas was very distressed that her martyrdom would be postponed because of her pregnancy – since, according to Roman law, pregnant convicts were executed only after delivery. She was afraid that she might have to shed her holy, innocent blood at a later time, separated from her Christian companions, and lumped in with others who were common criminals. Her companions in martyrdom were also saddened – they were afraid that they would have to leave behind so fine a companion – and that she would have to travel alone on the road to heaven.

Therefore, two days before the contest, they poured forth a prayer to the Lord in one torrent of common supplication. And immediately after their prayer the birth pains came upon Felicitas. She suffered a good deal in her labor because of the natural difficulty of an eight-month delivery. One of the prison guard assistants said to her, "You suffer so much now – what will you do when you are tossed to the beasts? Little did you think of them when you refused to sacrifice to the emperor." To this, she replied:

What I am suffering now, I suffer by myself. But when in the arena and professing my faith, the Holy Spirit will be inside me and will suffer for me, just as I will be suffering for Him.[57]

And she gave birth to a healthy girl. The sister of one of her companions brought her up as her own daughter. Two days later, Felicitas was executed in the arena.

MARTYRDOM OF UNMARRIED WOMEN SLAVES

THE virgin slave-girl martyr was probably equally motivated by faith, freedom, and virtue. Salvation, liberty, and morality (especially control over her sexuality) provided her with multiple reasons to escape from the dreadfulness of everyday life. Personal control over all aspects of one's life is a powerful motivation – an overwhelmingly powerful drive for some. *The virgin slave-girl died for faith, freedom, and virtue equally threatened.* Such a sensibility is found in the accounts of the martyrdoms of the slaves Seraphia, Blandina, Agathoclia, Laurentia, Flora, Lucilla, Dula, and others.

Seraphia and Sabina – between 110 and 125 AD

There was a Christian family who fled from Antioch in Syria to Rome to escape the persecutions of the emperor Hadrian. However, shortly after arriving in Rome, the parents died and the daughter named Seraphia (also called Serapia or Seraphima) was left to fend for herself. Although offers of marriage were many, Seraphia was drawn to a religious life, and she resolved to consecrate herself to God alone. So, she sold all her possessions and distributed the proceeds to the poor. Then she sold herself into voluntary slavery, and entered the service of a widowed Roman noblewoman, named Sabina.[58] As the slave of a noblewoman, she was safe from exploitation. Sabina and Seraphia formed a bond of mutual respect and understanding, and at some point, Sabina, who had been evangelized by Seraphia, was converted to Christianity, and they became involved with the local Christian community.

However, the comings and goings of the pair with the underground Christian movement did not escape the attention of the local governing officials. Eventually, they were captured, arrested, and tried for confessing to be Christians. Seraphia was denounced as a witch and commanded to do homage to the pagan gods of Rome. But she refused and was handed over to two shameless young men of Egyptian descent, who tried to rape her. But Seraphia resisted so forcefully that the villains despaired, and then to punish her defiance, they tried to set her on fire by placing her over a burning wood pile. But the fire would not injure her body, as she called on the mercy of God. Exasperated, the reprobates appealed to the local judge Berillus for a ruling on the punishment. Believing that she was a sorceress, the judge ordered her to sacrifice to the Roman gods for forgiveness. But Seraphia remained steadfast and refused. By official decree, then, she was beaten with sticks and rods – but she could not be broken. Amazingly, splinters from the sticks struck Berillus in his right eye, and after three days the tormentor became blind in that eye. Still unable to exact a confession, Seraphia was then executed by beheading. Her body was taken by Sabina and buried in her own tomb.

Being of noble birth, Sabina was spared and warned not to pursue this dangerous religion. But she was so disconsolate over losing Seraphia, that she continued to befriend the Christians. Less than a year later, Sabina was again denounced – as a criminal found aiding and abetting the Christians. This time there was no leniency. When the judge Helpidius questioned her, she humbly confessed,

Christ is my God; I adore Him and serve Him; to Him alone I must sacrifice.

With that, she was summarily executed for her faith by beheading – and all her assets were confiscated. She was buried in the tomb that she herself had built, and where she had interred her beloved servant, Seraphia. The two women soon became revered by the local Christian community.[59]

Blandina and the Martyrs of Lyons – 177 AD

One of the worst persecutions Christians faced in the early centuries occurred in the province of Gaul in Vienne, near Lyons, under the reign of Marcus Aurelius. In the year 177 AD, the wrath of the governor, the military, and the populace was exceedingly aroused against a group of

Christian believers, including the 90-year-old sickly bishop of Lyons, the deacon of Vienne, and other prominent followers. The entire congregations of two churches were rounded up, their assets seized, and the believers thrown into prison. False charges of orgies, incest, and cannibalism were trumped up and levied against them. Becoming exceedingly indignant and exasperated, the community soon became outraged and demanded confessions and penance. Having these kinds of people in their community, close to their children and homes, was just unacceptable. Those who would not renounce their faith, and accede to the good and proper Roman deities, were punished by torture and execution. Among this group of martyrs were three women: a slave named Blandina, her mistress and owner, and a woman named Biblias.

The mistress was concerned over Blandina's bodily weakness, thinking that she would not be able to withstand the physical tortures and make a bold confession of faith. The other members of the group were also afraid that she would succumb. But Blandina was filled with such power and conviction, that even those who were taking turns to torture her in every way from dawn to dusk, were weary and exhausted. She was hung on a post and exposed as bait for the wild animals that were let loose upon her, hanging there in the form of a cross. But by her fervent prayers spoken aloud, she aroused intense fervor and confidence in those who were undergoing their own ordeals – they were assured and would not waver.

For in their terror with their physical eyes, they saw in the person of their sister, He who was crucified for them – and that all who believe in Him and suffer for His glory, will have eternal fellowship in heaven with God Almighty.

Agathoclia of Aragon – 230 AD

Agathoclia was a young unmarried Christian slave owned by two people in Aragon, Spain, named Nicolas and Paulina, who had left Christianity and converted back to paganism. They regularly subjected Agathoclia to physical abuse, including whipping and battering, not only in an effort to get her to renounce her faith, but also to reinforce their assumed superiority and her inferiority. But she consistently and humbly took the beatings in stride, and repeatedly refused to renounce her faith.

At some point, Nicolas and Paulina decided that Agathoclia needed to be publicly punished and humiliated. So, they had her subjected to a public trial by a local magistrate. They claimed that she was disobedient by willfully not obeying their orders – and she was charged with refusing to pay homage to the gods when commanded by her owners to do so.[60] But once again, she refused to renounce her Christian faith. This caused her to be subject to severe persecution from the Roman authorities, since they believed that Christians disrespected the gods. The harshness of the sentence included having her tongue cut out, in an effort to get her to stop verbalizing her beliefs. But Agathoclia was resolute, and continued to deny her accusers through hand signs and head waving. Consequently, she was given the full punishment of torture, mutilation, and execution. During the proceedings, Paulina poured hot burning coals on her neck, and then, in a fit of exasperation, threw Agathoclia into the fire pit.

NOTES

1. in Iconium, during Paul's First Missionary Voyage

2. Reference: Edward N Brown, *The Passion of Thecla: Faith and Fortitude* [Chicago:Crystal Sea Press, 2020]

3. Acts 17:34

4. In some traditions, the name Damaris means 'heifer', a young cow that has not yet given birth to a calf – in colloquial terms, a young girl.

5. Tradition holds that when he learned that Mary, the Mother of Christ, lived in Jerusalem, Dionysius travelled there from Athens to meet her. From this meeting, he is reputed to have said, "Her appearance, her features, her whole countenance testify that she is indeed the Mother of God." Later, he discovered where Mary departed this world to join her Son and her God – and he wept with torrents of tears. Since Mary died in 41 AD, Dionysius must have visited in the mid-to-late 30s, and would likely have been a ready-and-willing convert by the time Paul preached in Athens in 55 AD.

6. Cornelius Tacitus (trans. by J. Jackson), *The Annals of Imperial Rome and Agricola* (Books XIII–XVI) [Cambridge: Harvard University Press, 1937]. For a more modern reference, see: Ronald Mellor, *Tacitus' Annals* [Oxford: University Press, 2010].

7. Aulus Plautius was an aristocrat and commander of Roman Legions in Briton in 45 AD.

8. See Endnote #5.

9. "All the saints greet you, especially those of the emperor's household" - Philippians 4:22

10. although this is disputed by some scholars

11. This is unsubstantiated, but certainly believable since she was obviously prominent in the Roman Christian community.

12. Alphaeus is mentioned as being the father of the Apostle Matthew (Mark 2:14) and also the father of the Apostle James the Less (Mark 3:18 and Matthew 10:3), but scholars are divided in opinion as to whether Alphaeus, the father of Abercius and Helena, is the same Alphaeus who is the father of Matthew and/or of James the Less [there is also doubt as to whether it is the same man, or two different men with the same name, who is the father of Matthew and James the Less].

13. The location of the two tombs eventually became 'St. Peter's Basilica' and the 'Basilica of St. Paul Outside the Walls'.

14. The relics of Basilissa and Anastasia are at the 'Saint Mary Queen of Peace' church in Rome.

15. Titus Flavius Clemens was a cousin of the emperor Domitian, with whom he served as consul from January to April in 95 AD. Shortly after leaving the consulship, Clemens was executed, allegedly for atheism, although it was probably because he professed Christian leanings. He is regarded as an early Christian martyr.

16. The island of Pontia (modern-day Ponza) and its neighboring islands, Palmarola and Zannone, lie off Cape Circe on Italy's west coast about 100 miles south of the mouth of the Tiber River at Ostia, the ancient port of Rome. It is a narrow crescent of high limestone ridges descending in sheer cliffs to a series of coves with fantastical shapes. Some of these shapes appear in ancient paintings representing the episodes of Homer's Odyssey. The bay of Chiardiluna was important for religious reasons, since on the heights above it is an ancient major cemetery. The island was notorious in the Early Roman Empire as a place of exile for members of the royal family who were for one reason or another causing embarrassment at Rome. It was a high-end (but not too high-end) and remote (but not too remote) lodge for banished noblepersons. It was here that Nero, son of Germanicus, died after his imprisonment by Tiberius. And here was the villa to which Caligula banished his sisters.

17. 40 miles off Turkey's west coast, Patmos served as a Roman prison station, as did many other islands in the surrounding vicinity. It was austere and not a nobleman's abode like at Pontia in Italy. See Revelation 1:9.

18. 304 AD was the apex of the persecution.

19. Refer to 1 Corinthians 7:8-9 and 1 Corinthians 7:32-33.

20. Various Christian denominations hold different saints in veneration. In this book, Roman Catholic and Eastern Orthodox (mainly Russian, Greek, and Antiochian) saints are presented, with a scattering of prominent Coptic and Protestant individuals. A complete and exact compilation of all saints venerated in all Christian denominations is beyond the scope of this book, but a good reference source can be found at: Melissa Petruzzello, "List of Saints", Encyclopædia Britannica, September 2020, https://www.britannica.com/topic/list-of-saints-2061264, accessed January 2021.

21. The Desert Mothers represent the pinnacle of asceticism for women.

22. There is some overlap here with the 'Founders/Benefactors'.

23. *Daily Life in Ancient Rome* [Oxford: Blackwell, 1992]

24. Clive Skidmore, *Practical Ethics for Roman Gentlemen: the Work of Valerius Maximus* [Exeter, 1996]

25. Alan Watson (ed.), *The Digest of Justinian* [1985]

26. Reference Exodus 21, Leviticus 25, and Deuteronomy 15:21

27. Deuteronomy 24:15

28. quite possibly with the exception of the high religious leaders

29. Galatians 3:27-28 and 1 Corinthians 12:13

30. 1 Peter 2:18

31. 1 Timothy 6:1

32. Ephesians 6:5-6

33. Titus 2:9-10

34. Philemon 10-16

35. 1 Corinthians 7:24

36. 1 Corinthians 7:20-21

37. The second greatest commandment – see Matthew 22:39

38. Matthew 24:40-1

39. Luke 17:7

40. Acts 18:1-3

41. Acts 16:14

42. Philippians 4:22

43. As such, Callistus belonged to the imperial 'family of Caesar'. Denounced as a Christian, he was sentenced to hard labor in the mines of Sardinia. However, through the intervention of Marcia, Commodus' concubine, Callistus and his fellow Christians in the mines were set free. The letter of liberation was taken to the governor of Sardinia by an imperial messenger named Hyacinthus, who was himself a Christian presbyter. After his release, Callistus returned to Rome and was ordained as a deacon by Pope Zephrynius. In 217 AD, now a free-man, he succeeded him as Bishop of Rome and Pope.

From 217-221 AD, he exercised great influence in important Christian issues throughout the empire. During his reign as pope, the Church witnessed its first antipope when Hippolytus formed his own Christian community against Callistus, who he believed was too lenient on sinners. At some point, he was killed and then thrown into a well, but his body was rescued and today the relics of the sainted pope are located in the church of Saint Mary in Trastevere (Our Lady of Trastevere) in Rome. See: D. J. Kyrtatas, *The Social Structure of the Early Christian Communities* [London and New York: Verso, 1987].

44. Romans 16:10-11

45. Galatians 3:28

46. Pope Pius in the 2nd century and Pope Callistus in the 3rd century

47. 1 Timothy 6:1-4

48. There is a record that at the beginning of the fifth century, a wealthy Roman aristocrat (and later to be ascetic), Saint Melania the Younger, gratuitously granted liberty to thousands of slaves – so many that her estate lawyer was unable to give an exact number – some sources say 8000, but it may have even been more. Reference: M. Cardinale Rampolla del Tindaro, *Santa Melania giuniore, senatrice Romana* [Rome: 1905], p. 221.

49. Herbert Musurillo, *The Acts of the Christian Martyrs* [Oxford: University Press, 1972]

50. Francis Joseph Bacchus, "Eusebius of Caesarea", The Catholic Encyclopedia. Vol. 5. [New York: Robert Appleton Company, 1909].

51. A person at the very bottom of the totem-pole was the slave-girl Blandina. But she became one of the most heroic martyrs and saints ever. During her persecution and suffering, it was said that onlookers saw not just a woman being brutalized on a stake, but instead they saw the Christ, "He who was crucified for them, in the form of their sister." Paraphrased from: Eusebius, *Church History*, in *Nicene and Post-Nicene Fathers of the Christian Church*, vol. 1, trans. by Arthur Cushman McGiffert, ed. by Philip Schaff and Henry Wace [Grand Rapids, MI: William. B. Eerdmans, 1982].

52. The dating of Pliny the Younger's governorship is uncertain. It is known that he arrived in his assigned province in time for emperor Trajan's birthday celebrations on September 18 in a year which could be 109, 110, or 111 AD. He served a little more than two years and died in office. Thus, the letters could date from 109 to 113 AD.

53. In early Christian baptism ceremonies, catechumens were anointed and baptized naked, with a deacon accompanying them down into the pool of water. In the case of female catechumens, simple propriety would suggest that a woman would perform this task, since the anointing did not involve merely pouring oil over the candidate's head and shoulders, but was comparable to the way oil was used in Greco-Roman bathing and in athletic contests of the period – the oil was rubbed into the person's skin and over their whole body as a kind of quasi-mystical enhancement. When the baptized woman came up out of the water, the deaconess would instruct her in purity and holiness on how the seal of the baptism was unbreakable. Also, in the case of female Christians who were sick or otherwise homebound, it was proper for a woman to deliver communion (the Eucharist sacrament) to them, since it would usually involve visiting the woman in her bedchambers. See: John Wijngaards, *Women Deacons in the Early Church: Historical Texts and Contemporary Debates* [New York: Herder & Herder, 2006].

54. Betty Radice (ed.), *Pliny Letters, Books I–VII and Books VIII–X* [Cambridge: Harvard University Press, 1969]

55. Other Christians that Pliny had interrogated had recanted under threat of torture, but he could never be certain if they were just telling him 'what he wanted to hear' or the real truth of what was going on. Roman courts understood that torture was not always effective as a means for learning the truth of a case, since many people have the patience and endurance to be contemptuous of torture. The truth can never be extracted from them. On the other hand, others have so little patience that they would tell any kind of lie rather than suffer the torture. See: Alan Watson (ed.), *The Digest of Justinian* [1985].

56. Pamphylia is the ancient name for the fertile coastal plain in southern Anatolia between Lycia and Cilicia, extending from the Mediterranean to Mount Taurus (all in the modern-day Antalya province of Turkey).

57. Herbert Musurillo, *The Acts of the Christian Martyrs* [Oxford: University Press, 1972]

58. Sabina was the widow of a Roman senator named Valentinus and the daughter of a man called Herod Metallarius.

59. In 425 AD, a church was built over the site of the martyrdom of the two holy women, and dedicated to Saints Sabina and Seraphia (but now known simply as Saint Sabina's). By the 13th century, the church became the international headquarters of the Roman Catholic Dominican order. Even today, under the main altar, one venerates the bodies of the two holy martyrs.

60. This was a grave offense because if the gods were displeased, they could cause disasters and catastrophes on the society (draught, famine, earthquake, fire, pestilence, etc.). It was important that they be kept happy by providing the proper respect, reverence, and tribute. People that wouldn't do this had to be dealt with one way or another.

4 FREEDOM AND FAITH

Hope for a better life, a better future

The wild card in the game of life during the first few centuries AD, was the concept of personal freedom, and just how far an individual would go to get, or keep, that freedom. For both the slave and the young unmarried person, freedom was the release from bondage – the ability to make one's own decisions, take one's own actions without fear of reprisal, and live independently of society's unjust laws and customs; to be able to do what they wanted to do and not what someone else (or someone else's rules) wanted them to do.

For the slave, the desire for a free life meant the release from daily labor obligations – often arduous or backbreaking obligations – and the ability to pursue one's own occupational pursuits and dreams. For the unmarried female, the desire for a free life meant the release from the obligation of marriage (often to an undesirable and intolerant individual) and the release from the drudgery of wifely chores (in many cases, almost being a slave to her husband). It also meant the relief from the hazard and discomfort of childbirth. In both situations this also meant the liberation from beatings and punishments, since this was not uncommon among haughty arrogant slaveowners and husbands. For the unmarried female slave, the desire for a free life was triply attractive (not to be married, not to be bonded, and not to be destined to spiritual death.)

In a culture where one's possibilities in life were largely predetermined by class, wealth, and gender, freedom presented the opportunity to obtain a degree of individual control. Even if people could not change the political, social, or economic structures of the world, they could change their behavior. Especially for women, a life of celibacy delivered them from some of the undesirable constraints normally imposed upon them. A life of virginity also meant that the risks of childbirth were avoided. Ancient women suffered from complications at childbirth far more often than is the case for women in industrialized countries today. Lastly, celibate women had opportunities for meaningful work and service usually not available to married women.

If freedom is the wild card in the game of living, then faith is the wild card in the eternal game of life – physical life before death, and spiritual life after death through resurrection of the body. Some slaves wanted only freedom from their oppressive owner and cared not about faith. Likewise, some women wanted freedom from an oppressive marriage and cared not about faith. These secular concerns had always existed throughout history – and there had always been various escape methods, although not very good ones. But the new religion of Christianity now presented a new opportunity – one that looked promising – a new escape route with a chance for freedom. And a freedom that would last forever!

Many formerly non-religious people embraced the faith, hoping that this would be their pathway to freedom. However, this particular pathway was fraught with danger.

The new religion was illegal, and persecution was often swift and deadly. Was this new religion the answer? What good was it to be free if you were dead or maimed? Was it really worth the risk?

Most of the victimized decided that it wasn't. There were other avenues whereby one could attain freedom that were less dangerous – buying your way out with money, or running away and hiding (hoping to find someone who would shelter you long term), for example. But these options were just not feasible for most. Consequently, most of the victimized stayed where they were – slaves remained slaves and unmarried maidens got married and became wives. Some lived a happy life, but many did not.

Curiously, a good percentage of the slaves and unmarried young women decided to embrace the new religion of Christianity, despite the risks. They decided to take the plunge and commit themselves to the new lifestyle, knowing full well that they could be found out, persecuted, and even killed. After all, if found, exposed, and charged with a crime, they could always just recant, change their mind, beg forgiveness, and promise to go back to the life that they had before. Sure, there might be some recrimination, but in time it would pass and everything would be just as it was before. So why not take the chance – give it a shot?

However, the Christian faith was different from all the other escape routes, since it alone was based predominantly on love and freedom. It enabled a self-worth and self-esteem, regardless of social status. And it forgave all sins of the past with love and compassion. At the same time, it humbled the individual, yet made everyone feel that they were an integral part of something bigger; like being part of an important team – a movement.

But most importantly, it gave the person hope – hope for a better life, a better future. And not just hope for this life, but hope for everlasting life. This hope was possible because of the gift of grace – a free gift that is given to everyone, slave or free, male or female, married or unmarried – the forgiveness of sin and the promise of life everlasting. All that was required in return was a sincere effort to be pure of mind and body – and belief in God Almighty, in Jesus Christ our savior, and in the Holy Spirit. The ceremonies were simple, yet emotionally powerful – lifting them up and making them want to be better. The believers craved the ceremonies – it reinforced their beliefs and made them feel spiritually restored and physically healthier.[1]

This was a faith that appealed to the marginalized and the under-trodden, but was available to everyone. It provided what all the other escape routes failed to provide – a vision of future happiness – individual freedom and the blessing of togetherness with loved ones, in an everlasting life of peace and joy, in community with God, the angels, the saints, and all who have been saved.

But was this new religion worth the risk – worth losing everything for – worth dying for? For the vast majority, the answer was YES. In fact, once baptized into the faith, their commitment was generally unwavering. The potential rewards just outweighed the risks. The human desire for love and freedom is just too great to be stifled by earthly machinations.

Indeed, there were some who left the faith, brought about heretical ways of thinking, or tried to instigate unholy activities. The apostle Paul, himself, complained about them.[2] But at the same time, he praised all those who stood by him and remained true to the faith.[3]

In the centuries after Paul, the church grew and matured, the catechism developed, and the liturgy refined. The doctrinal heresies grew more complex and disagreements over the theological details continued to sprout. But the number of people who joined the faith, and found it to be fulfilling, just kept increasing – and the geographical reach just kept expanding.

Young and old, rich and poor, slave and free, married and unmarried – they all came in search of something better – an alternative to what they had. And most of them, once converted, remained committed. Their absolute moral determination to follow the precepts of the faith is amply illustrated by the phrase:

We cannot live without Sunday (or more explicitly, *without the Sunday Eucharist*)

The phrase originated with the martyrdom of the 49 Martyrs of Abitinae, who were murdered in 304 AD when emperor Diocletian prohibited Christians, under penalty of death, to possess Christian books (the Sacred Scriptures), convene on Sunday to celebrate rituals (the Holy Liturgy), or erect premises for their assemblies.[4]

The judge at the trial asked one of the accused, Octavius Felix, the following question: "I am not asking if you are a Christian, but if you have taken part in their assembly, or if you have a book of their teachings?".

To this question, Felix replied, "With due respect, your honor, that is a foolish and ridiculous question! I tell you that a Christian cannot live without the Sunday Eucharist – and the Sunday Eucharist cannot be celebrated without there being a Christian present. It is the Sunday Eucharist which makes the Christian, and the Christian that makes the Sunday Eucharist – so that one cannot exist without the other, and vice versa."

Of course, the judge was not amused. He couldn't understand the reasons for their commitment since he was unwilling to learn the precepts of the faith. To him, it was just another dangerous radical cult that needed to be eradicated. Members of most of the other radical cults he had dealt with usually recanted when faced with torture and death. But for some reason he didn't understand, these Christians were different. Nevertheless, if the cult members insisted on disobeying Roman law, then they had to pay the price, regardless of gender, marital status, how many, how young, how old, how rich, how poor, how intellectual, or how industrious. It didn't matter. Octavius Felix, and 48 others (including ~20 women and 4 children [1 infant son]), were put to death for refusing to renounce their faith (more specifically, for refusing to worship the Roman pagan gods and idols).

Even severing the bond of family wasn't a sure way to force the Christians to change their ways and renounce their faith. There are many cases of sons and daughters refusing the pagan religion of their parents, and even of siblings going their own separate ways. During the time of persecution of emperor Valerian, two Christian women, named Rufina[5] and Secunda, who were daughters of a Roman senator, were betrothed to two Christian men named Armentarius and Verinus. When serious persecutions began in 257 AD, Armentarius and Verinus renounced their faith. But Rufina and Secunda remained stalwart, refused to renounce, and went into hiding. The men became indignant and, along with the father, helped the authorities locate and capture the women. When their father, in presence of the judge, asked them directly about their religious persuasion, intimating that a wrong answer could have deadly consequences, they responded:

My dear father, you can do with me as you wish. You can even take my life. But you have no power to take the faith of Jesus Christ, my Savior, out of my heart. He will strengthen me to suffer patiently all that you have threatened.

But the father, and the fiancés, would not intercede or plead on behalf of the sisters. Rufina and Secunda were found guilty, tortured, and finally beheaded.[6] Such it was with many families. Freedom to pursue one's faith frequently trumped all other concerns.

BY THE NUMBERS

THERE were a great many young women who chose celibacy, chastity, and martyrdom over life in a dismal marriage with a pagan or overbearing husband. The numbers spike during the worst persecutions, as described in chapter 2. The following table gives a snapshot of the relative numbers of female saints who were considered martyrs, virgins, and slaves prior to 313 AD):

Category of Saint	Number (approx.)
All saints in heaven today	(only God knows)
Recognized by Christian denominations	more than 10,000
Who died before 313 AD	more than 1000
women	200
unmarried young women (virgins)	120
Who were martyred before 313 AD	800
women	180
unmarried young women (virgins)	115
Who were slaves, martyred before 313 AD	unknown

women	20
unmarried young women (virgins)	10

Notes:

1) For each category, an unknown number of unnamed individuals that fit that category, that are included in large group martyrdoms (ex. the martyrs of ....), must be added to these numbers. Unfortunately, these group martyrdoms often have an estimated or inaccurate number of individuals.

2) In addition to the inaccuracy of group martyrdoms mentioned in Note 1, there are many other causes for indetermination. For example, this number could exclude biblical figures who died prior to the birth of Christ, or to the start of His ministry. In addition, there are likely duplicates, which should be excluded, where names have been mixed up with other individuals with similar names, comparable situations, or close-together timeframes. Finally, angels and archangels could also be excluded.

3) For the category 'unmarried young women (virgins)', the focus is on young women who chose celibacy and chastity, rather than marriage and child-bearing/rearing, due to religious conviction, at a time in their life when societal expectations demanded otherwise. This was a critical decision that she had to make – and one that the woman knew could have dreadful consequences. In this context, 'unmarried' is synonymous with 'virgin'. Historically, young unmarried girls were called 'virgins', especially in the area of martyrology. It would be unthinkable for an unmarried girl to be otherwise – certainly not saintly.

4) It should be pointed out that there are many cases of older celibate and chaste women who dedicated themselves to a consecrated or ascetic life, and are recognized as saints (ex. The Desert Mothers). They are not to be under-appreciated.

5) In many cases, the distinction between slave and servant is unclear, so the categorization reflects a best understanding of the situation. Also, prizes of war are considered as slaves.

GROUP MARTYRDOMS

IN many instances the persecutions involved large groups of individuals. This usually occurred when there was a systematic or institutional 'round-up' of Christians or suspected Christians. The following table is a list of group martyrdoms where women were included (or where it's possible that women may have been included). In many cases, the actual number of martyrs is unknown, or the number of women martyrs is unknown. Excluded are group martyrdoms where only men were involved (to the best of our knowledge). If the name of a woman in a group is known, then she was included in the appropriate chapter of this book. Note that the number of slaves or virgins within a large group was often unrecorded.

Group	Year	Place	Number

First Martyrs of the Church of Rome
  Neronian Martyrs
  Protomartyrs of Rome
	64-68	Rome	Dozens of disciples of the Apostles with scant historical evidence; number of women unknown

The Martyrs of Pamphylia	127-138	Attalia, Pamphylia	Family of 4; 1 woman
Symphorosa (or Felicitas) and her 7 Sons	138 or 164	Tivoli, Italy	Family of 8; 1 woman
The Nonuplet Sisters	139	Portugal	9 women
The Martyrs of Vienne and Lyons	177	Lyon, France	50 martyrs; at least 3 women (+ 1 male child)
The Scillitan Martyrs	180	Carthage, N Africa	7 men; 5 women
10,000 Martyrs of Mount Ararat (number questionable)	250	Armenia	converted Roman soldiers; number of women unknown but very small
Massa Candida (martyrs thrown in pit of burning lime)	253-260	Utica, N Africa	300 martyrs; number of women unknown (reduced to mass of white powder)

The Theban Legion (number uncertain)	286	Gaul	number of women unknown but very small
Hripsime, Gayane, and the 33 Virgins	290	Armenia	35 women
Demiana and the 40 Virgins	302	Egypt	41 women
Countless Martyrs of Zaragoza (Saragossa)	303	Zaragoza, Spain	1st group: 17 men, 2 women 2nd group: number unknown
Martyrs of Samosata	286-305	Samosata, Syria	7 martyrs; number of women unknown
30 Martyrs of the Appian Way (soldiers)	304	Rome	number of women unknown but very small
Martyrs of Abitinae (Albitina)	304	Carthage, N Africa	49 martyrs; at least 20 women (+ 4 children [1 infant])
Donatus, Romulus, Secundian, and 86 Companions	304	Venice, Italy	89 martyrs; number of women unknown
10,000 Martyrs of Nicomedia (number questionable)	303-309	Nicomedia	number of women unknown
Adrian, Natalia and 23 Companions of Nicomedia	306	Nicomedia	24-25 martyrs; Natalia uncertain; number of women unknown

NOTES

1. To this day, many religious groups suggest offering a sacrifice (attending mass or service with communion) three times a week (often Wednesday, Friday, and Sunday) as a good practice for the lay person.

2. See 2 Timothy 4:10,14-16.

3. See 2 Timothy 4:19-21

4. After the Last Supper, Jesus instituted the Holy Eucharist, the sacrament and sacrifice of His Body and Blood. Refer to Matthew 26:20-29. The offering of bread and wine, as the transubstantiation of Christ's body and blood, is the Catholic tradition of this celebration.

5. No relation to Claudia Rufina mentioned in Chapter 3.

6. The bodies of Rufina and Secunda were buried on the Via Aurelia, and the 'Church of Saints Rufina and Secunda' was built in their honor in Rome.

5 THE EXALTED HEROES

Their names, lives, and stories must not be forgotten

THE HEROIC BLANDINA:
SAINT, MARTYR, VIRGIN, SLAVE

<< *Salutation and Opening of a Letter to the Faithful* >>
(see Introduction)

The greatness of the tribulation in the regions of Gaul near the towns of Vienne and Lugdunum, and the exceeding anger of the local heathens against our holy believers, and the sufferings which the blessed witnesses for Christ endured, I am not competent to describe accurately, nor is it possible to detail it all in writing. For with a mighty strength the devil did assault the servants of God, using all sorts of tricks, deceptions, and prevarications. By this, all the local citizens were stirred up against us – not only were we excluded from forums, baths, and markets, but it was forbidden for any of us to be seen in any public place.

But, by the grace of God, the holy believers remained steadfast, enduring all forms of shame and injury – the weak were rescued and the strong stood like firm pillars against the shaking. With courage and integrity, the witnesses for Christ firmly kept the faith, maintaining that 'the sufferings of the present time are nothing compared with the glory that awaits us in heaven'.

At first, we nobly endured all the harms and vices that were heaped upon us by the local citizenry – hooting, catcalls, beatings, robberies, stoning, and everything that an infuriated mob is willing to inflict on those whom they consider to be unworthy and derelict. At length, many of the servants of God were forcibly taken to the police station by soldiers, and brought before the magistrates that had charge of the town. They were questioned in presence of the public, and having confessed to being Christians, they were locked up in prison until the arrival of the governor.

When finally brought before governor Saturninus, he displayed a marked spirit of hostility toward them. However, a local citizen of high moral and ethical standards, named Vettius Epagathus, who had the full measure of love towards God and his neighbors, was very concerned that unreasonable judgments might be passed against the believers. Strong in spirit, eager to serve, and moved with passion, he petitioned for a hearing in defense of the others. His goal was to show that there was nothing ungodly or impious among them. But the jurors in the court were not interested in listening, and the governor, oblivious to his request, simply asked him if he was a Christian himself. And on his confessing in the clearest voice that he was indeed, he also was taken up into the number of the accused, receiving the designation 'Advocate of the Christians', and sent to the prison. He was a genuine disciple of Christ and a role-model for the others.

The first group of arrested believers were then brought in, and the governor announced to them, "You can win the indulgence of our lord the emperor, if you return to a sound mind."

Sanctus, a deacon from Vienne and the de-facto spokesman for the group, replied: "We have not done anything wrong, and we have not been part of any wrongdoing. Our minds are sound. We have never spoken ill to anyone, but when ill-treated we have given thanks in return. This is because we respect our emperor and our empire."

Saturninus interrupted, saying, "We too are religious, and our religion is simple. We swear by the genius of our lord the emperor, and pray for his welfare, as you also ought to do."

To which Sanctus replied, "If you will sincerely listen to me, I can tell you about the mystery of our faith."

But Saturninus was not so inclined. "I will not listen to you once you begin to speak evil things about our sacred rites. Swear to me in the name of our lord the emperor, that you will not do this."

"The empire of this world I know not," responded Sanctus. "Rather, I serve the true God, who no man has ever seen, nor with these eyes can ever see. Honorable sir, I have not committed any theft or deceit – whenever I have bought anything, I have paid the tax. But I know that my Lord and my God is the King of kings and the Emperor of all nations."

"Enough of this prevarication," said Saturninus, "I have heard enough." Then turning to the others, he stated straightforwardly, "You must all cease being of this unholy persuasion."

But Sanctus countered, "But it is an unholy persuasion to torture, murder, and speak false witness, is it not?" (implying that that was the persuasion followed by the Romans).

"Be not partakers of this folly," reiterated Saturninus sternly and impatiently, with the air of intimidation.

Then, another member of the accused named Maturus, a recent convert, said "We fear no one else except our Lord God, who is in heaven."

He was joined by Attalus, the pillar and foundation of the church in Pergamum,[1] who said, "Honor is to Caesar as Caesar, but reverence is to God as God." [2]

Then Sanctus said simply, "I am a Christian."

"And you still persist in being a Christian?" asked the governor.

"I am a Christian," Sanctus repeated.

"What I am, is what I wish to be," said Maturus.

"And I am a Christian, and wish to be a Christian," stated Blandina, the only woman in the group. And with them, all the rest affirmed the same.

"Would any of you be inclined to reconsider that position?" asked the governor.

Sanctus' answer was short and quick: "In a matter so straightforward, there is no considering."

After a few moments of pondering, Saturninus asked, "What are the things in your suitcase?"

"Books and letters of Paul, a just man."

Then the governor said, "Have a delay of seven days and rethink your answers."

But Sanctus promptly said a second time, "I am a Christian." And with him they all agreed.

Then, after taking a deep sigh, the governor Saturninus read out the decision and sentence to the jurists and onlookers: "Sanctus, Maturus, Attalus, Blandina, and all the rest – having willingly confessed that they live according to the Christian customs, and since after opportunity offered them of returning to the correct and proper custom of the Romans, they have obstinately persisted to refuse; it is determined that they be imprisoned, and then sent to the arena at the proper time to be subjected to the tribulations therein as punishment. However, because the magnanimity of the emperor is boundless, the opportunity to avail themselves of a proper confession that honors the traditions and customs of Rome will remain in effect throughout the period of confinement and punishment."

To which they all replied, "We give thanks to God."

After this, the rest of the accused began to be examined and questioned in groups. Most of the believers were strong in their faith and openly confessed that they were Christians. But some were unprepared and nervous about the repercussions. Of these, about 10 in number renounced their faith, causing immeasurable sorrow among the rest of the believers. But they were not permitted to walk away. All of the accused were confined together (the persecutors hoping to spread dissension among the ranks). However, those who had confessed were worried about the durability of the confessions, dreading that one could fall away and deny his faith because of the pressures.

More and more servants of God were being apprehended daily, filling up the number of the accused. All the pious members of the two churches, together with the founders, leaders, and financial backers, were rounded up and cast in the prison. Even some heathen household slaves belonging to the well-to-do church members were apprehended, since the governor had given orders that all the Christians should be sought out (and the use of informers [finger-pointers] was one way to do this).

Urged on by the soldiers and fearing the pain and tortures that the believers were facing, most of the slaves falsely accused the believers of cannibalism, incest, and other crimes which are unlawful to mention, or even think of. Of course, no such crimes had ever taken place, but the damage was already done simply by the accusations. When the rumors were spread about, all the people raged against the servants of God like they were the dregs of the earth – any that were formerly temperate in their conduct toward the believers, now became exceedingly indignant and condescending toward them. Thus, the prophecy of our Lord was fulfilled: *Not only will they expel you from synagogues; a time will come when anyone who puts you to death will claim to be serving God.*"[3]

Then, over the course of the next few days, the holy servants of God were sent two-by-two into the arena, where they suffered tortures beyond all description. To an exceptional degree, however, the wrath of the people, as well as the soldiers, fell on Sanctus, Maturus, Attalus, and Blandina. The thinking was that if the leaders could be rehabilitated or eliminated, then the rest would fall in line and the problem would go away.

Blandina was the wild card in all of this. Sanctus, Maturus, and Attalus were strong, healthy, and vigorous, but Blandina was weak, ill, and unfit. Being a simple uneducated slave, her leadership capabilities were disregarded. But the spirit of God was extremely powerful in her. For the things that appear to most humans to be ugly and contemptible, may in fact be beautiful and noble to God. Although frail, sickly, unsightly, and worthless on the outside, because of her love for God, Christ gave her the traits of goodness and beauty on the inside – strength, purpose, virtue, integrity, honesty, and morality were hers in abundance. And the righteousness of Blandina expressed its true glory at this sorrowful time.

Her owner (mistress) was one of the accused, and she was concerned that Blandina would not be able to withstand the tortures and maintain a bold confession of her faith, because of the weakness of her body and the meekness of her personality. But her inner strength was massive and soon became apparent to all. For while the rest of the servants of God were afraid of the pain, and of falling away in the faith, Blandina was filled with such upright power, that those who tortured her one after the other, in every way from morning until evening, were wearied and tired, confessing that they were completely baffled at her grit, bravery, fortitude, and courage. When they had no more tortures that they could impose on her, they were astonished that she remained alive, even though her whole body was broken, mangled, gashed open, slashed, punctured, and pierced. The tormentors gave their testimony that only one of the modes of torture inflicted should have been sufficient to deprive her of life, not to mention the excruciating pain and suffering. But the blessed Blandina, like a noble athlete with the power of God, recovered her strength and composure after each torture, and never renounced her faith. At each stage of the tribulations, she would proudly declare, "I am a Christian, and there is nothing vile done by us."

Sanctus also nobly endured all the horrible and ghastly tortures that were thrown against him. The persecutors hoped, because of the continued severity of the tortures, that he would renounce his faith and admit to the unlawful practices. But Sanctus withstood them with firmness – he would not even tell them his own name, nor that of his birthplace or residence, nor if he were slave or free. But in answer to all these questions, he simply said, "I am a Christian." That was the statement he made repeatedly, in reply to every question that was put to him. Because of this perceived arrogance, the governor and the torturers determined that a quick execution was needed. So finally, they affixed red-hot plates of brass to the most delicate parts of his body, and burned him continuously and intensely. With that, the body of Sanctus became charred, misshapen, and limp. But he remained alive, and never recanted his beliefs.

In suffering for the faith, Christ brought about great wonders, destroying the devil, and showing a heroic example to the faithful that there is nothing to be feared when God's love is present – and nothing painful when Christ's glory is imparted. After a few days, the persecutors again tortured the servants of God, thinking that since their bodies were battered, bruised, swollen, and inflamed, if they were to apply the same torture instruments again, this time with the ultimate consequence of death hanging over them, they would be able to coerce them into giving up and renouncing their beliefs. This would also demoralize the rest of the believers. But no such occurrence took place. Blandina and Sanctus were immutable. And all the rest of the servants of God were inspired.

Among those who had denied Christ during the initial interrogations was a woman named Biblias. The devil, thinking that he had already swallowed her, and wishing to damn her still more by making her accuse falsely, brought her forth to punishment. Physically constraining the already feeble and spiritless woman, the persecutors endeavored to force her to utter accusations of cannibalism against the believers. But, in the midst of the tortures, Biblias awoke from her stupor and came again to a clear state of mind. For the temporary suffering reminded her of the possibility of eternal punishment in hell, and she contradicted the accusers of the Christians, saying, "How can children be eaten by those who do not even think it lawful to taste the blood of spiritless animals?" And then she reversed her denial and confessed herself to be a Christian – and was added back to the number of believers.

When the tyrannical tortures were found to be insufficient to force the servants of God to renounce their beliefs, the tormentors devised other dreadful and despicable contrivances – such as confinement in the darkest and dirtiest parts of the prison, stretching of the feet to the fifth hole in the stocks, and other indignities that torturers are accustomed to inflicting on prisoners, when stirred by the devil. The result was that a great many believers expended themselves and died in prison, being chosen by the Lord for this manner of death. But there were others who were tortured so bitterly, that it seemed impossible for them to survive even if nursing had been provided. Yet they remained alive in prison, destitute of human attention, but strengthened by the Lord, and invigorated both in body and soul. These heroes consoled and encouraged all the others. But the poor souls of many of the newly converted, the just recently apprehended, and the ones whose bodies had not been previously tortured, could not endure the confinement torment, and they died in the prison.

At this time, the blessed bishop of Lyons, named Pothinus, was brought into the courtroom by soldiers of the tribunal, accompanied by the civil magistrates and a multitude of people who shouted affronts, slurs, and offences against him in every conceivable manner, as if he were the embodiment of Christ himself. He was now upwards of 90 years of age, and exceedingly weak in body. Though he breathed with difficulty on account of his body's feebleness, he was strengthened by the eagerness of his spirit to give an earnest testimony in defense of the believers. Although his body was worn out by old age and disease, the life energy was preserved within him, such that Christ might triumph through him.

When asked by the governor who the God of the Christians was, he quietly said, "If you are worthy, then you will know and understand." That didn't go over well, and he was subsequently dragged away harshly, receiving many blows from the soldiers and the spectators. Those onlookers nearby struck him with their hands and feet, irrespective of his age, while those at a distance hurled all sorts of insults against him, each one thinking that he would be guilty of great wickedness in the eyes of the gods if he omitted any possible abuse. Sadly, they thought that by doing this, it would please their gods. Scarcely able to breathe, Pothinus was cast into prison, where he died two days later.

Now at this time, a certain great dispensation of God's providence occurred. The persecutors decided to imprison those apostates, who upon their initial arrest had denied Christ, together with all the servants of Christ who had confessed their belief, and force them to share in the confinement and hardships. Their denials, in fact, turned out to be of no advantage to them. For while those who confessed were imprisoned simply as Christians (no other accusation being brought against them), those who denied were detained as murderers – corrupted, degraded, and dishonored – and they faced punishments twice as severe. As a result, the deniers were tormented greatly by their own consciences, so that when they were led forth into the arena, their countenances were easily distinguishable from all the others, being downcast, humbled, sad-looking, and weighed down with every kind of disgrace. Moreover, they were even reproached by the local pagans as being base and cowardly. They had lost all honor, status, and reputation.

On the other hand, the confessors were lifted up by the joy of their testimony, and their hope in the promises of Christ. They went into the arena rejoicing, glory and grace being blended in their faces, so that their chains lay like sparkling ornaments around them. And they were perfumed with the sweet savor of Christ, such that they seemed to be anointed with the world's finest ointment. When they realized the fate of the deniers, they felt sorrow for them, but their hearts were strengthened knowing that the devil had no place in their own thoughts.

Then, in short order, all the accused were paraded into the arena and forced to endure the tortures until death overcame them. Their punishments were different, but the end result was always the same.

Sanctus and Maturus were publicly exposed to the wild beasts,[4] in order to give the heathen public a spectacle of cruelty that is commonly used for hard-core criminals. Like athletes who had overthrown their adversary several times and were now contending for the crown, they again endured the torments which beat upon them. They were dragged about by the wild beasts, and suffered every indignity which the maddened spectators demanded through cries and shouts. And finally, they were placed in the iron chair, on which their bodies were roasted until they were filled with the fumes of their own flesh. But the torturers did not stop there, becoming ever more frantic in their desire to overcome the stamina of the Christians. While the whole time, the only thing that was heard from Sanctus was the same four words, over and over again, that he had uttered at the beginning: "I am a Christian."

Sanctus and Maturus remained alive the entire day throughout the gruesome contest, presenting an extraordinary show for the arena spectators that was much different than the usual gladiatorial combats. But at last, their lives were sacrificed, their bodies broken beyond recognition. But their will and their faith were never shattered. And so, Sanctus and Maturus went to be with their Maker, our God and Creator, wearing the holy crown of martyrdom.

Attalus was in great demand by the people for a spectacle in the arena because he was a person of notoriety, one that epitomized the immorality of the Christians. He accepted the punishment with clear conscience, entering the contest readily as a true witness for Christ. In an effort to demean him to the point of utter humiliation, he was paraded slowly around the arena, a sign being carried before him on which was written, '*This is Attalus the Christian*', causing the people to be swelled with indignation against him. The boos and hoots in the arena were deafening. But when the governor learned that he was a Roman citizen, he ordered that he be taken back to prison and kept with the other Roman citizens who were already there awaiting a final determination of their fate.[5]

Blandina was hung up fastened to a stake in the ground, and exposed as food to the wild beasts that were let loose upon her. But because of her earnest prayers, and because she appeared as if hanging upon a cross in a manner similar to our Savior,[6] she inspired the servants of God with great zeal. For in their terror with their physical eyes, they saw in the person of their sister, He who was crucified for them – and that all who believe in Him and suffer for His glory, will have eternal fellowship in heaven with God Almighty.

When none of the wild beasts would touch her, she was taken down from the stake and conveyed back to prison, thus preserved for another contest. But unrealized by the wicked torturers, this was an omen of fresh hope for the believers, encouraging them to remain strong and true to the faith – a shining light in the darkness. For though she was a feeble, pathetic, and despised woman, yet she was clothed with the great and invincible armor of Christ. She would continue to overpower the enemy, and in the course of the contest, would win for herself the crown of righteousness.

After this, there was a lull for a few days as the arena was cleaned up and readied for the next spectacle. This intervening time turned out to be uplifting to the servants of God – through their tenacity and perseverance, the immeasurable love of Christ was made manifest. For through the living, the dead were made alive – through the love of the confessors, the deniers were moved to confess. There was great joy among the believers in receiving back those who they thought had been lost. Most of those who had denied returned to the church and were reinvigorated in the faith.

Being now restored to the fold, and having their spirits uplifted, they went back to the courtroom to be again questioned by the governor. For our merciful God desires not the death of the sinner, but the repentance and penance of the sinner. This new examination took place because the emperor had decided that the accused-and-sentenced confessors should be punished, but that if any of them changed their plea and denied being Christian, then they should be set free.

Now, at this time, a public festival was beginning, that was attended by crowds of people from all over the empire. The governor had the confessors, the blessed servants of God, brought to the judgment podium set up in the arena, exhibiting them as a theatrical show to the unruly spectators. And they were examined and questioned again. Those who refused to deny were sentenced to death by beheading if they possessed Roman citizenship. If they were not Roman citizens, the sentence was death by being set out as prey for wild beasts.

The original deniers were also brought to the judgment podium in the arena, the intent being that if they still denied, they would be set free, and that would demonstrate the benevolence of the emperor. But contrary to expectations, most of them now confessed, and were added to the group of believers, where they were brought back to the church. Unfortunately, there remained a few who continued to deny. They had lost their faith and their love of God – love of self had taken precedence. They continued to disparage the servants of God by giving false reports and blaspheming the

Christian way of life. May God have mercy upon their souls.

Present at these examinations was a man named Alexander, a native of Phrygia,[7] and a physician by profession. He had lived for many years in Gaul, and had become well known for his love of God and his boldness in proclaiming the truth. He stood near the judgment podium, and encouraged (by hand and body signs) those who had denied to confess. But the people were becoming angry because so many of those who had formerly denied, were now confessing. So they cried out against Alexander, as if he was the cause of their change of heart, demanding that he be removed. Sensing the tension in the air, the governor summoned Alexander before him, and inquired just who he was. When Alexander replied that he was a Christian, the governor became angry and summarily condemned him to the wild beasts. He was scheduled for the next day in the arena along with Attalus, who the governor wished to expose again in order to gratify the boisterous crowd.

And the next day the two servants of God were tormented in the arena with all the instruments devised for that unholy purpose. After having undergone exceedingly severe tortures, the pair were at last slain, to the delight of the crowd. Alexander neither groaned nor shrieked in any manner, but communed in his heart with God until the end. But when Attalus was placed on the iron chair, and the fumes rose from his burning flesh, he shouted to the people in the crowd, "Listen to me – what you are doing here is devouring people, but we Christians do not do any such thing, or any other wicked thing for that matter." Then, some people in the stands who were smirking asked him, "What is the name of your god?" And Attalus replied just shortly before expiring, "God has not a name like mortal people have."

On the last day of the gladiatorial shows, Blandina was brought in again along with Ponticus, a boy of about 15 years of age. The two had been taken every day to the arena to watch the tortures that the others had to endure, and they were pressured to renounce their faith at every opportunity. But because they remained steadfast in their confessions, the raucous crowd became incensed – and they had no pity for the youth of the boy nor respect for the sex of the woman.[8]

Accordingly, the torturers put them through all the terrible sufferings, and inflicted upon them the entire gamut of tortures; exposing them to every brutal terror, repeatedly trying to compel them to deny their faith. But they failed. In the end, encouraged and reassured by his sister-in-Christ, and after nobly enduring every kind of inhuman cruelty, Ponticus gave up the ghost and went to be with his Maker in heaven.

The blessed Blandina was the last of them all to suffer through the array of tortures and torments orchestrated by the devil and inflicted on the servants of God. After having been like a noble mother encouraging her children to remain strong, keep the faith, love God with all their hearts, and anticipate the resurrection and eternal life in heaven, she too had to face the end game. And this she did with grace, honor, and integrity, never yielding an inch to the servants of the devil. In progression, she was scourged with whips and rakes, mauled by wild beasts, and roasted in the iron chair. Finally, she was enclosed in a net and thrown onto the horns of a frenzied bull. Her body gored, pierced, and broken apart from being tossed wildly about, she was at last impaled in a most horrific manner.

The heathens themselves acknowledged that never among them had a woman endured so many and such terrible tortures.

Thus, the heroic Blandina was the last of the martyrs of

Lyons to receive a crown of righteousness. To the very end, her faith, hope, and love for Christ never wavered. She knew that the others were looking to her for inspiration and encouragement, and she knew that she couldn't let them down. Even during the final excruciating moments of torture, her thoughts were not on the pain, but on the role of helper that had been entrusted to her by God – how her purpose in life was to provide comfort and assistance to others in helping them find their way to the Light through a maze of darkness – to find the true path to God, salvation, and everlasting life, even when hopelessness and despair appeared to be overwhelming obstacles.

Martyr, saint, virgin, slave: Blandina was all of the above. In her 16 odd years of life on earth, she achieved the fullest measure of sanctity, rising from an earthly state of paucity to a divine state of abundance.

Alas, the story of what happened here is not yet complete. Even after the close of the spectacle, the madness was not yet ended, and the cruel hatred was not yet appeased. The fact that the persecutors had been rebuffed in their attempt to force the believers to renounce their faith, did not put them to shame, but rather just intensified their anger. Both the officials and the people continued to exhibit an unjust hatred of the servants of God, in fulfillment of the Scripture: "Let the wicked continue in their wicked ways, the depraved in their depravity! The virtuous must live on in their virtue and the holy ones in their holiness!" [9]

The directed violence of the persecution found another evil opportunity in the dead bodies of the believers. They threw to the dogs those who had been suffocated in prison, carefully watching them day and night, so that the bodies couldn't be retrieved and buried. They laid out the mangled remains left by the wild beasts and the scorched remains left by the fire. In like manner, they placed the heads of the decapitated next to their bodies, and left them lying unburied for many days, watched by a military guard. There were some passersby who cursed and spat at the remains, seeking to get from them further vengeance. Others laughed, mocked, derided, and insulted them, at the same time propping up their own idols, and giving them the credit for punishing the Christians. There were also people of a milder disposition, who seemed to sympathize, but they could usually be heard muttering, "So where now is their God, and what good has their religion done them? Why would they choose this in preference to their life?" Such was the thinking that characterized the conduct of the heathens.

But our state was one of deep sorrow because we could not bury the bodies of the martyrs. The darkness of night aided us not – the guards were too vigilant. Bribery failed to persuade – the little money that we had wasn't enticing enough. And pleading and begging was to no avail – the guards had been commanded, under penalty of death, to keep the watch. The officials believed that their final victory over the Christians was in not allowing the remains to be buried.

The bodies of the martyred servants of God, after having been mistreated in every possible manner, were left exposed in the open air for six days, accessible to the grisly pickings of birds and scavengers. Then they were burned with fanfare and reduced to ashes. Unquestioning workers swept all the ashes into the river Rhone, which flows past, such that no trace of them might appear on the earth.

They did these things so as to prevent the martyred souls from being resurrected (which they had been told would occur), and then snatching victory from defeat – having the last laugh, so to speak. Even though they scoffed at the idea of a resurrection, the pagan officials had to cover all the bases – they couldn't allow any chance happening, no matter how unlikely, from seizing their victory away from them. They had to make absolutely sure that the vile Christian religion was crushed for good. While all of this was going on, they could be heard snickering, "Now let us see if they will rise again, and if their God is able to help them by delivering them out of our hands."

I am writing this letter to make sure that the world remembers these events, learns from them, and is changed for the better, in the name of Jesus Christ, our Lord and Savior. And so, altogether, 50 believers and servants of God were crowned with martyrdom in Gaul at this time, but Blandina, the virgin slave, was the most heroic of them all. In the Name of the Father, and of the Son, and of the Holy Spirit, may they rest in peace forever and ever. Amen.

May God have mercy on the world.

Your humble servant in Christ.

< *signature appended* >

[end of letter]

THE HEROIC PERPETUA AND FELICITAS: SAINT, MARTYR, MOTHER, SLAVE [10]

<< *Salutation and Opening of a Letter to the Faithful* >>
(see Introduction)

The citizens and officials in the areas surrounding the great city of Carthage in North Africa, spurred on by the devil, have instigated an attack on the blessed followers of Christ, that have left us saddened beyond words. But at the same time, we have become stronger as a community because of the strength and fortitude of our holy believers, both those who stood firm against the accusers face-to-face, and those who encouraged and supported them from afar. It's difficult for me to describe the terrible sufferings that have been imposed upon us, but believers everywhere need to know what happened here, so they can understand and prepare for similar onslaughts in the future. But our will is unbreakable. Because the anguish we suffer in this world, is nothing compared to the glory that awaits us in the next.

In Carthage, we had a vibrant Christian community that included a great and wise man named Tertullian.[11] Those drawn to our growing church came from all backgrounds; young and old, rich and poor, slave and free. The Roman emperor, Septimius Severus, had forbidden conversion to Christianity or Judaism, and the local governor, Hilarianus, seeking self-advancement in the eyes of the emperor, decided to enforce this edict. Out of the blue, five of our holy believers were arrested, in clear violation of the emperor's edict, since they all were only catechumens (people preparing for baptism), and not yet officially converted. The three men arrested were named Saturninus, Secundulus, and Revocatus, a slave. The two women arrested were named Vibia Perpetua, 20-year-old daughter of a prosperous provincial family, and Felicitas (nicknamed Felicity), a slave. Perpetua had just given birth to a baby son only two weeks earlier, and Felicity was eight months pregnant. Yet no leniency was afforded either of them because of their conditions. Another Christian who voluntarily turned himself in and joined the small group, was named Saturus, their instructor in the faith.

Perpetua's pagan father was frantic with worry and tried to talk her out of her decision. As a well-educated, high-spirited woman, she had every reason to want to live – including the infant who she was still nursing.[12] But her answer was simple and clear. Pointing to a water jug, she asked him, "See that water jug over there? Can you call it by a name other than what it is?"

"Of course not," her father answered.

To which she responded, "Neither can I call myself any name other than what I am – a Christian."

This answer so upset the father that he moved angrily toward her as if to strike her. But he caught himself at the last moment, stepped back, shook his head, and stormed off in a huff.

Just before being taken to the holding prison, the five catechumens were baptized in our faith. It was a deep source of encouragement for them all. Perpetua was known for her gift of receiving messages from God and relating them to others. After the baptism, she said that she was inspired by the Spirit to ask for only one thing – endurance for all in the face of their trials and sufferings.

A few days later, the holy believers were moved to the prison, a terrible place – dark, dirty, hot, and crowded with criminals and traitors. The guards and soldiers pushed and shoved them around without any concern, just like all the others. It was a dungeon. Felicity was in much discomfort, suffering from the stifling heat, overcrowding, and rough handling while being eight months pregnant. But she remained stoic.

The next day, two deacons of the church, Tertius and Pomponius, bribed the prison guards to allow our righteous captives to be moved to a better part of the prison, where they could have visitors. Perpetua's mother and brother were able to come and bring her baby to her, and she was comforted. She was even given permission to keep the child with her in prison for a day, although I think she was pained because she felt her mother and brother suffering out of pity for her, and the trials she would have to endure.

Her brother then said, "sister, you are greatly privileged; surely you might ask for a vision to discover whether you are to be condemned or freed."

Perpetua promised that she would speak to the Lord. This she did – and her resulting vision was revealed to all the believers.

< see Appendix III for the narrative of Perpetua's dream, part 1 >

After listening to Perpetua's dream, the believers knew that suffering was their fate, and that from then on, there was no hope left for them in this life – all their hope was now in the next life.

A few days later, Perpetua's father came to visit her, worn with worry, and attempted to convince her to renounce her confession. She remembered the interaction very vividly because it was very emotional. She told it all to the others, and these were her words:

"My father pleaded with me. 'Daughter,' he said, 'have pity on my grey head – have pity on me your father – if I deserve to be called your father, if I have favored you above all your brothers, if I have raised you to reach this prime of your life. Do not abandon me to be the reproach of men. Think of your brothers, think of your mother and your aunt, think of your child, who will be missing you once you are gone. Give up your pride! You will destroy all of us! None of us will ever be able to speak freely again if anything happens to you.'

"This was the way my father spoke out of love for me, kissing my hands and throwing himself down at my feet. With tears in his eyes, he no longer addressed me as his daughter, but as a woman. I was sorry for my father's sake, because he alone of all my kin would be the most unhappy to see me suffer. I tried to comfort him by saying, 'It will all happen in the prisoner's dock, as God wills – for you may be sure that we are not left to ourselves but are all in His power.'

"Unable to persuade me to change my conviction, he left in great sorrow."

Two days later, our respected accused were suddenly hurried off for a hearing. Word had spread throughout the neighborhood that a special event was to be held at the Forum, and a huge crowd had gathered. The believers were escorted, one by one, up to the prisoner's dock, a station with an elevated step in plain view of all the crowd. In turn, each was questioned, and without a second thought, each confessed to being a Christian.

When Perpetua's turn came, her father jumped out of the crowd with her son in his arms, pulled her off the step, and begged, "Recant your confession – perform the sacrifice – have pity on your baby!"

Hilarianus, the governor, said to her, "Have pity on your father's grey head; have pity on your infant son; offer the sacrifice for the glory and welfare of the emperor."

"I will not", Perpetua replied.

"Are you a Christian?" said Hilarianus.

"Yes, I am," she said.

When her father persisted in trying to dissuade her, Hilarianus became exasperated and ordered him to be thrown to the ground and beaten with a rod. I'm sure Perpetua felt sorry for father, just as if she herself had been beaten.

Then, sentence was passed on all the holy believers. They were condemned to death in the arena – to do battle with the wild savage beasts – and were then returned to the prison. Perpetua asked that her father bring her the baby, so she could continue with the nursing, but he refused, and she was grieved.[13]

In addition, Felicity was greatly troubled, both physically and spiritually. The labor pains were increasing and the day of birth was drawing near, but it was against the law for pregnant women to be executed, since killing a child in the womb was like shedding innocent and sacred blood. Felicity was afraid that she would not give birth before the day set for execution. In that case, she would likely be separated from her companions, and they would go on their glorious journey to heaven without her. Worse yet, she might have to shed her holy, innocent blood at a later date – this time along with common criminals, thieves, and deserters. She was very distressed. The other believers were worried that they might have to leave such a good friend and fellow believer behind, and then have her go into the arena later without their support.

A few days later, the warden in charge of the prison, named Pudens, had a change of heart, and began to show more kindness and respect to the holy believers, thinking that they possessed some great power from the gods. He allowed many visitors to see them for their mutual comfort. It was at this time that I was privileged to meet these heroes in person.

However, the military officer in charge was not so inclined. He treated them with contempt and harsh words because he had listened to foolish people, stirred by the devil, who warned him that they could be magically whisked out of prison by spells and incantations from sorcerers of their cult. He refused to move them to cleaner quarters.

Perpetua spoke to him directly. "Why can't you allow us to refresh ourselves properly? For we are the most distinguished of the condemned prisoners, seeing that we belong to the emperor. We are to fight on his very birthday. Would it not be to your credit if we were brought forth on that day in a healthier and fairer condition?"

The officer became embarrassed at her reproach, and gave the order that they were to be more humanely treated. And so, he also allowed friends and family to visit, and even to dine together.

Perpetua's father came, overwhelmed with sorrow. He

started tearing the hairs from his beard and threw them on the ground. Then he threw himself on the ground and began to curse his old age, crying and wailing with very emotional and moving words. Perpetua was very sad but remained steadfast in her convictions.

Two days before the contest and execution, two events occurred that drove the believers from the depths of despair to the heights of joy. Secundulus was called from this world to be with God in the middle of the night, while suffering from ill health, the cold, and the unsanitary conditions. Everyone was very grieved. We believe now that it was by special grace from God – that he might not have to face the final tortures.

Felicity was also suffering a great deal in her labor. So, the holy believers poured forth prayers to the Lord in one long torrent of common grief and supplication. And immediately after their prayers, the birth pains came upon her, and she went into a difficult labor. The guards derided and insulted her by saying, "If you think you suffer now, how will you be able to stand it when you face the wild beasts in the arena?"

Felicity answered them calmly, saying, "What I am suffering now, I suffer by myself. But when in the arena and professing my faith, the Holy Spirit will be inside me and will suffer for me, just as I will be suffering for Him."

And minutes later, to the ecstasy of all, she gave birth to a healthy baby girl. God is good, alleluia! One of the Christian sisters of the accused adopted her, and brought her up as her own daughter.

The day before they were scheduled to confront the beasts in the arena, Perpetua had a vision, and afterwards shared it with the group.

< see Appendix III for the narrative of Perpetua's dream, part 2 >

On that last day, the holy believers were paraded out in front of the public for their last meal (called the free banquet). It was a feast day before the day of the games in the arena – so that the crowd could see the prisoners and make fun of them. But our holy believers turned it all around – they didn't grovel or plead for mercy – instead, they openly addressed the crowd, warned them of God's judgement (stressing the joy they would have in their suffering for Christ), scolded them for persecuting the Christians, and ridiculed those who called them atheists or perverts. They exhorted the crowd to follow their example and accept the Lord Jesus Christ.

Saturus, the teacher, said, "Will not tomorrow be enough for you? Why are you so eager to see something that you dislike? Our friends today will be our enemies on the morrow." He then added somewhat sarcastically, "But take careful note of what we look like now, so that you will recognize us in our glory tomorrow." Many of the people in the crowd were roused to think twice about the Christians, and whether their religion had any merit. It is hoped that such thinking could help lost souls find the Kingdom of God in the future.

When the day of reckoning arrived, the noble servants of God were forcibly marched from the prison to the arena. But they did not resist the deliverance. On the contrary, they seemed joyful, as though they were going to heaven – with calm faces, trembling with anticipation rather than fear. Perpetua walked with shining countenance and calm step, as a beloved of God, and as the wife of Christ – counteracting everyone's stare by her own intense gaze upwards. With them also was Felicitas, glad that she had safely given birth so that now she could fight the beasts – going from one bloody situation into another, from the birther to the gladiator, ready to wash herself again for God's glory.

They were led up to the entrance gate and the men were ordered to put on the robes of a priest – but not a holy priest of God, but rather a worshipper of the pagan Roman god Saturn. Likewise, the women were ordered to wear the dress of a worshipper of the pagan god Ceres. But the noble Perpetua vigorously objected to this:

"We came to this state of affairs of our own free will, such that our freedom would not be violated – the freedom to worship and sacrifice who and how we choose. We willingly agreed to trade our lives for our freedom – freedom to never do what you now tell us to. By condemning us, you agreed to this trade. You cannot now change the rules set forth under the laws of the Empire. Let the world know that the rule of Caesar is being abused here! We will not wear the robes of your idols!"

Perpetua's defense was so eloquent and powerful, that even the governor Hilarianus decided to relent on this issue. And the military tribunal agreed. So, they were brought into the arena in their normal civilian clothes. Perpetua then began to sing a psalm, while Revocatus, Saturninus, and Saturus began to shout sayings from Christ to the on-looking crowd. When they came before the imperial booth where Hilarianus was seated, they yelled with accompanying gestures: "You have condemned us, but God will condemn you".

At this, the throng of spectators became enraged, and demanded that they be scourged before a lineup of gladiators. This didn't faze our holy believers, as they imagined that they were sharing in the sufferings of our Lord. They endured the whippings gracefully and were then led back to the section of the arena where the wild beasts were kept.

Saturninus had maintained throughout the incarceration

that he wanted to be exposed to all the different beasts, so that his crown of martyrdom might be all the more glorious. And sure enough, at the outset of the contest he and Revocatus were matched with a leopard – and then while in the stocks, they were attacked by a bear.

As for Saturus, he was matched with a wild boar. But the gladiator who had tied him to the animal was himself gored by the boar and died a few days after the contest. Saturus was dragged about but was otherwise unhurt. Then, when he was bound in the stocks and awaiting the bear, the animal refused to come out of the cage. So, Saturus was returned to the staging area.

For the two young women, the tormentors had prepared a mad heifer.[14] They were stripped naked, placed in nets, and brought out into the arena. Barely able to walk, Felicitas had to be carried most of the way, and then dropped off like a lame goat. But even this contemptuous crowd was horrified when they saw that one person was a frail delicate woman and the other was a sickly young woman fresh from childbirth. They yelled with disapproval. And so, the pair were brought back again to the staging area, dressed in unbelted tunics, and returned to the arena.

The heifer first went after Perpetua, tossed her up in the air and she fell on her back, knocking the wind out of her. Sitting up slowly, she discovered that she was not seriously injured. And then, astonishingly, she pulled down the tunic that was ripped along the side so that it covered her thighs, thinking more of her modesty than of her pain. Next, she asked for a pin to fasten her untidy hair – for it was not right that a martyr should die with her hair in disorder, lest she might seem to be mourning in her hour of triumph.

Then, getting up, she saw that Felicity had been crushed to the ground by the beast. So, she went over to her, gave out her hand, and lifted her up. Although they were bleeding and bruised, the two proud women then stood up side-by-side, grasped hands, raised them up in triumph; and faced the spectators staunchly, looking up to heaven. The crowd cheered loudly, but they wanted more blood. So, the two were brought back to the gate for preparation for the next ordeal.

At the gate, Perpetua was met by a young man who was also a catechumen, but not yet arrested. She seemed to be in a daze, probably from a combination of the jolts from the heifer and her own pensive swooning. To the amazement of all, she said, "When are we going to be thrown to that heifer, or whatever it is?" When told that it had already happened, it wasn't until she noticed the telltale marks of the rough experience on her body and on her tunic, that she believed. Then, she called for her brother, and spoke to him together with the unarrested catechumens, saying: "You must all stand fast in the faith and love one another – do not be weakened by the suffering that we have gone through, and that we will yet go through." We were all so proud of this noble woman, and wished that we could share in her glory.

At another gate, Saturus was addressing the friendly officer they had met earlier, named Pudens: "It is exactly as I foretold and predicted. So far, not one animal has touched me. So now you may believe me when I say that I am going in there now to be finished off with one bite of the leopard." And sure enough, at that moment a leopard was let loose, and ran to attack Saturus, who had gone through the gate into the arena. Mauled by the bite of the leopard, and drenched in blood, he staggered away while the crowd roared their approval. "Well washed! Well washed!" they cried out, not understanding that to us, this was like a second baptism – this time in blood, as a sacrifice to honor our Lord and Savior.

Back at the gate, he said to Pudens, "Good-bye, my friendly jailor. Remember me, and remember the faith. These things should not disturb you, but rather strengthen you." With this, he asked the officer for a ring from his finger, and dipping it into his own wound, gave it back to him, saying, "This is a pledge that you remember what happened here, as a record of the blood shed for the faith." And officer Pudens accepted the pledge.[15]

Our blessed men had fainted from their wounds, and the gladiators made ready to finish them off by cutting their throats. But the frenzied crowd shouted for their bodies to be brought out into the open arena, so that their eyes might be the guilty witnesses of the sword that pierced their flesh and terminated their existence – and the people could readily witness the final dispensation of the hated Christians. And so, the holy martyrs were beaten back into consciousness and paraded out to the center, together with Perpetua and Felicitas.

They were all together for the last time, bloodied, broken, and bruised. Hugging one another, they sealed their martyrdom with the ritual kiss of peace. One-by-one, they took the sword in silence, looking upward without moving. Saturus was the first to die, being the oldest and the teacher.

Perpetua was the last. She screamed as she was struck on the collar bone by the sword.[16] But the wound was not fatal. The young novice gladiator didn't know what to do. He was so nervous, he could barely hold the sword in his trembling hand – it was wandering all over the place. So, in an act of utter grace, Perpetua took the shaking hand of the young soldier, and guided the sword to her throat.

It was as though so great a woman, feared as she was by the devil and the enemies of Christ, could not be dispatched unless she herself was willing.[17]

The Holy Spirit has permitted the story of this contest to be written down, to carry out the commission of our most holy saints and martyrs, and I am unworthy to add anything to it. This glorious story must be remembered exactly as it happened.[18]

O, most valiant and blessed martyrs! Truly are they called and chosen for the glory of Christ Jesus our Lord! Any man who exalts, honors, and worships God's glory should read, for the consolation of the Church, these deeds of heroism, which are no less significant than the deeds of a century ago. For these new manifestations of virtue bear witness to the one and the same Holy Spirit, to God the Father Almighty, and to His son Jesus Christ our Lord, to Whom is the power and the glory for all the ages. Amen.

May God have mercy on the world.

Your humble servant in Christ.

< *signature appended* >

[end of letter]

THE HEROIC THREE SISTERS:
AGAPE, CHIONIA, AND IRENE

<< *Salutation and Opening of a Letter to the Faithful* >>
(see Introduction)

Citizens of the city of Thessalonica in Macedonia, which is the hometown of emperor Diocletian's once junior emperor (or 'caesar') Galerius, have initiated a harsh attack on our saintly believers and on our precious holy scriptures. It was Galerius who first persuaded Diocletian to commence an empire-wide persecution of Christians (so it is not surprising that the persecution is especially severe here).

It was just this year (303 AD) that Diocletian published

an edict forbidding, under pain of death, any person to keep Christian doctrinal or liturgical books (the Holy Scriptures). Now, the believers concealed many volumes of these sacred books, but rumor spread among the citizens that certain people had obtained them unlawfully and were worshipping them. It wasn't long before seven of the faithful were accused by a pagan traditionalist of not following the edict. The names of the accused were Agape, Chionia, Irene (who were sisters), Casia, Philippa, Eutychia, and Agatho (being the only man). The seven were rounded up and brought before the provincial governor Dulcetius for trial. The official accusation was primarily, that they refused to eat meat as a sacrifice to the Roman gods, and secondarily, that they were hiding Christian books, that were supposed to have been surrendered for destruction.

Seated confidently in his court, the governor nodded to the secretary Artemesius to begin the proceedings.

"Your highness, if you please, I will read the testimony provided by the constabulary concerning several persons here present."

To which Dulcetius replied: "Let the information be read."

"Based on the information provided by the reputable citizen and senior pensioner Cassander, the constabulary presents to you six Christian women and a man, who have refused to eat meats as a sacrifice to our revered gods. They are named Agape, Chionia, Irene, Casia, Philippa, Eutychia, and the man's name is Agatho. Therefore, they are brought before you for judgment and ruling."

Turning to the women, Dulcetius said harshly, "What wretched madness is this of yours, that you will not obey the pious commands of the emperor and the caesar?" Then, without waiting for an answer, he looked at Agatho and asked more passively, "Why will you not eat of the meats offered to the gods, like other subjects of the empire?"

"Because I am a Christian," replied Agatho.

Dulcetius frowned, and then asked him again, "And do you still persist in that statement?"

"Certainly," was Agatho's reply.

Dulcetius then looked directly at Agape, saying: "What are your sentiments?"

She answered, "I believe in the true living God – and I will not lose all the merit of my life by any evil action that you may administer."

Then the governor said, "And what say you, Chionia?"

"I believe in the true living God", she answered, "and I follow His orders before any other's."

He then turned to Irene and said, "Why did you not obey the most pious command of our emperors?"

To which she answered, "For fear of offending the true living God."

"And what say you, Casia?" he continued.

" I desire to save my soul," she said matter-of-factly.

"Will you not partake of the sacred offerings?"

"By no means."

Then he turned to Philippa and said, "And as for you, Philippa, what do you say?"

"I say the same thing," she answered.

"And what is that?"

"That I would rather die than eat the food that you sacrifice to idols. I sacrifice only to the true living God."

"And you, Eutychia, what do you say?"

"I say the same thing," she replied, "I would rather die than do what you command."

The governor then took a different tact. Continuing to look at Eutychia, he asked, "Are you married?"

"My husband has been dead almost seven months now," she replied.

"And by whom are you with child?"

"By him who God gave me for my husband."

Staring very intently at Eutychia, Dulcetius then said in a very stern voice, "Listen to me closely Eutychia. For the good of your child, as well as for yourself, I strongly advise you to disassociate yourself from this folly, and resume a reasonable way of thinking. So, what do you say? Will you obey the imperial edict?"

"No, for I am a Christian," she responded, "and I only serve the one true living Almighty God."

With that, governor Dulcetius made a decision and gave a pronouncement: "Being far along with child, let the woman Eutychia be kept in prison until such time that the case can be reviewed again." It wasn't that he was altruistic. Roman law prohibited the execution of pregnant women, for the simple reason that the empire needed warm bodies.

After an hour rest break, the governor called forth Agape, and said, "Agape, what is your final declaration? Will you do as we do, who are obedient and dutiful to the emperors?"

Her answer was succinct. "I will not obey commands from the devil. Get behind me Satan! My soul will not be overcome by the evil intent driving these dialogues."

Shrugging his shoulders and shaking his head, he then turned to Chionia. "And you, Chionia, what is your final answer?"

"Nothing can change me," she replied.

The governor thought for a moment, and then said, "Do you have some books, papers, or other writings, pertaining to the religion of the impious Christians?"

"We have none now," Chionia retorted, "All that we once had has been confiscated from us."

He continued by asking, "Who drew you into this immoral persuasion?"

"The one true Almighty God," she said.

Hoping to get damaging information on other Christian subversives, he repeated the question: "Who convinced you to embrace this folly?"

But her answer was unchanged, "Almighty God, and his only Son, our Lord Jesus Christ."

That ended the questioning. Dulcetius had heard enough. After a few minutes' reflection, he issued his final verdict and sentence.

"You are all bound to obey our most glorious emperors and caesars (junior-emperors). But because you have willingly and continually despised their just commands, along with our suggestions, rebukes, reprimands, and warnings – and have had the boldness and rashness to adamantly ignore these admonitions, retaining the irreverent name of 'Christians' – and since to this very moment you have not obeyed the constables and officers who solicited you to renounce this Jesus Christ in writing – you shall receive the just punishment you deserve."

Sensing that Agape and Chionia were the leaders behind the disobedience, he then read their sentence: "I condemn Agape and Chionia to be burned alive at the stake, for having out of malice and stubbornness acted in contradiction to the divine edicts of our lords, the emperors and caesars; and who at present continue to profess the false and immoral religion of the 'Christians', which all pious people detest and abhor."

Then he added: "As for the other four, let them be confined in a secure prison until such time that I deem appropriate for reconsideration."

Two days later, our beloved saintly believers Agape and Chionia were burned to death without fanfare or ceremony. May their holy spirits forever rest in peace in heaven. Their sacrifice shall not be forgotten.

Two days after that, governor Dulcetius brought Irene back into court for further questioning. It seems that in the interim, the police had discovered some Christian books in her possession. By confronting her with this evidence, he hoped to convince her to recant and give sacrifice to the gods – or failing that, to get her to implicate other Christians, including her own father.

"Your madness is plain, my deluded child, since you have been found keeping to this day many books, pamphlets, and tracts unique to the ungodly Christians. You were previously required to acknowledge them when questioned thereupon, but you lied and denied that you had anything. It seems that you will not take warning from the punishment of your sisters – neither have you the fear of death before your eyes. Your punishment therefore is unavoidable.

"However, the grace of the empire is magnanimous. I will not refuse even now to make some condescension on your behalf. Therefore, notwithstanding your crime, you can be pardoned and freed from punishment, if you will yet worship the great gods of Rome. What say you then? This is your last chance. Will you obey the orders of the emperors? Are you ready to pledge obedience to the gods, and make the sacrificial offering?"

To which Irene calmly replied, "By no means will I do that – for those that renounce Jesus Christ, the Son of God, are doomed to eternal fire."

Giving up on the fate of Irene, Dulcetius decided to concentrate his efforts on obtaining information that could help the empire in the capture and punishment of other devout members of our 'Way', who he considered enemies of the state. So, he pressed Irene with further questions:

"Who persuaded you to conceal those books and papers

from us for so long?"

"Almighty God," she responded, "who has commanded us to love him even unto death. Therefore, we will not betray him – we choose to suffer any punishment whatsoever, rather than allow our sacred writings to be confiscated and defamed, belittled, or destroyed."

The governor continued to press. "Who knew that those writings were in the house?"

"Nobody, but the Almighty, from whom nothing is hidden. We concealed them even from our own servants, lest they should expose us and accuse us."

"Where did you hide yourselves last year, so that you couldn't be found when the virtuous edict of our emperors was first announced?"

"We went into the mountains, where it pleases God."

"And with whom did you live?"

"We were out in the open in makeshift shelters, sometimes in one place, and sometimes in another."

"Who supplied you with bread?"

"Almighty God, who gives food to all flesh."

"Was your father privy to this?"

"No, he had no knowledge of any of it."

"Which of your neighbors knew about this?"

Irene's response was stiff-lipped: "Inquire yourself in the neighborhood, make your own search, and draw your own conclusions."

But Dulcetius persisted. "After you returned from the mountains, as you say, did you read those books to anybody?"

"They were hidden in our house, and we dared not touch them and open them. Because we could not read the holy words day and night as we had been accustomed to doing, we were greatly distressed and anxious. We became distraught and troubled."

Realizing that he could not extract any useful

incriminating information from her, governor Dulcetius issued his final sentence: "Your sisters have already suffered the punishments for which they were condemned. As for you, Irene, since you were condemned to death before this latest crime of hiding these books before the just eyes of the empirical magistrates, your punishment must be greater and entail even more suffering. You do not deserve to die quickly or mercifully. Therefore, I order that you be left exposed naked in a brothel, and open to whatever depravities exist in that place. You are allowed only one loaf of bread a day, and the guards will prevent any escape from your cell, under penalty of death to them."

Irene was led away to a low-end brothel to serve her sentence. As per the decree, she was left naked in a cell and subject to all the worst debaucheries imaginable. Many wicked unscrupulous men, and even some women, came to her cell. But in all cases, no matter how offensive, depraved, or licentious the intruder was, Irene enraptured and mesmerized them with a saintly radiance that was gifted to her by God. None of them felt compelled to force any immoral or indecent advances on her, and they all left the cell contented – praise the lord – thanks be to God.

After three days, the governor caused her to be brought again before him

"Do you still persist in the rashness of your beliefs?" he asked.

"Not in rashness of belief, but in eternal belief of total piety towards God," she replied.

"Then it is settled," decreed the governor, "You shall suffer the just punishment for your insolence and obstinacy."

Then he imposed the official sentence: "Since the woman Irene will not obey the emperor's orders and sacrifice to the great gods of Rome, but, on the contrary, persists still in the irreverent and wicked religion of the 'Christians', I order her to be immediately burned alive, as her sisters have been."

That very day, she was seized by the soldiers of the court and brought to a high mound of ground where the executions were commenced. Having lighted a large pile, they ripped off her clothes and tied her to the stake. Singing psalms and celebrating the grandeur of God, the glorious martyr Irene was there-and-then consumed in the fiery inferno. Now she is with our Lord and God in heaven. May she rest in peace, the saintly Irene.

These events occurred in the ninth term of emperor Diocletian, and the eighth of caesar Maximian, to which I attest as an outside but informed party to the events.

May God have mercy on the world.

Your humble servant in Christ.

< *signature appended* >
[end of letter]

NOTES

---

1. At the urgings and persuasions of empirical bureaucrats, many people from the Roman towns and cities in Asia Minor relocated to France to help bolster the economy there, and to present a stronger front to the barbarians of the north (the Germans and Burgundians being the greatest threats) who might have ideas about incursions into the territory of the empire. Many of the Christians in the area of Lyons had family roots in Asia Minor, where they had originally been Christianized. Pergamum was an ancient Greek city in Mysia, about 16 miles from the Aegean Sea. It is now the modern town of Bergama in the province of Izmir in Turkey.

2. Compare this to Jesus' answer to the duplicitous spies in Luke 20:20-26.

3. John 16:2

4. They first were compelled to run the gauntlet, a track filled with traps, tricks, tortures, and torments, which was the custom at the time, before fighting with the wild beasts.

5. The governor had written to the emperor questioning what the policy was for dealing with the Christians, and was awaiting an answer.

6. In Roman society, crucifixion was the usual form of punishment commonly inflicted upon slaves and the worst criminals. Roman citizens, no matter how wicked, were exempt from this indignity.

7. Phrygia was a large inland district of Asia Minor, comprising most of the central Anatolian plateau. Much of it was annexed to the Roman province of Asia in 116 BC, but some portions were incorporated within the provinces of Galatia and Cappadocia.

8. Although Blandina and Ponticus were approximately equal in age, Blandina was clearly much more mature. In fact, Ponticus looked up to her as an older and wiser sister.

9. see Revelation 22:11

10. As should be clear from the text, Perpetua was from a rich, well-to-do family, the daughter of prosperous provincial parents. Felicitas (or Felicity) was a slave, although the owner is unknown.

11. Tertullian (155–240 AD) was a prolific early Christian author. He was the first writer to produce an extensive collection of Latin Christian literature and apologetics.

12. Perpetua was properly married, but her husband and her younger brother had recently died (some accounts say that the husband was out of town).

13. Perpetua had been nursing the baby, even when in the prison, and thought that she had to continue. However, in actuality, the baby's desire for breast milk had waned, so her concern for the child's welfare was relieved.

14. A heifer is a young female cow that has not yet mothered a calf. These animals had proved to be especially vicious toward human females.

15. This is not the same person as Saint Pudens, mentioned in 2 Timothy 4:21, who was baptized by Saint Peter and martyred under emperor Nero. 'Pudens' was a common Roman name meaning 'modest'.

16. Some sources say she was stabbed between the ribs.

17. Saints Perpetua and Felicity, watch over all mothers and children who are separated from each other because of war or persecution.

18. Perpetua kept a diary that vividly described her trial and imprisonment. Details describing her death in the arena were added by a friend after the horrible events. This accounting of heroic martyrdom has been highly revered by both ancient and modern Christian scholars. Her text is one of the rare surviving documents written by a woman in the ancient world. Perpetua's diary was read annually in Carthage's churches for centuries. It was so influential that it was praised by orthodox and heretical Christians alike. 200 years later, the Church Father Augustine (354–430 AD) wrote sermons commenting on the young martyr's words. This account, known as "The Passion of Sts. Perpetua, Felicitas, and their Companions", was so popular in the early centuries that it was read during church liturgies. This powerful text, with its emotional and personal voice, continues to draw readers today. For reference, see: "Acts of Perpetua and Felicitas" in *The Ante-Nicene Fathers*, Philip Schaff (ed.), Marcus Dods (trans.), [Peabody, MA: Hendrickson Publishers, 1996]. Most scholars agree that Tertullian authored the work, using the prison diaries and letters of Perpetua and Saturus as resources, around 230 AD. Also see Thomas J. Heffernan, *The Passion of Perpetua and Felicity* [New York: Oxford University Press, 2012].

6 THE HEROIC UNMARRIED WOMEN

Saint, Martyr, Virgin

This chapter is a summary of the most famous, noble, virtuous, and heroic virgin martyrs in chronological order. The truth of the matter, is that in reality, these women have the greatest (most sensational) recorded stories, and not that they were the greatest (most famous, noble, virtuous, or heroic) of all the virgin martyrs. The real truth behind the stories is lost to history, but of course not to God.

BALBINA THE VIRGIN – ROME (~130 AD)

As a military official in the Roman army, Quirinus had been ordered to hold Pope Alexander I,[1] and a Roman governor named Hermes, in prison because of their Christian faith leanings. They were held in separate prisons that were a great distance apart, and both were shackled and well-guarded. Quirinus was trying to convert Hermes back to the old gods, but promised to become a Christian if Hermes could prove that there was an afterlife. Hermes explained that Pope Alexander could make a better argument than he, and asked several times to visit his prison. At first Quirinus agreed to this, but after a while he became angry, convinced that these visits were frivolous excursions. He then stopped the visits and tightened the guard so that the two would not be able to speak with one another. That night, Hermes prayed to God for assistance, and in reply, an angel appeared to Pope Alexander, released his chains, and brought him to Hermes' prison cell.

The next morning Quirinus came to Hermes cell as usual, and was shocked to find both men inside. His heart now softened to what the two Christians had to say, he stayed and talked with the men for a long while. Hermes shared his story of how Alexander, with the help of God, had raised his son from the dead. Hearing this, Quirinus said that his daughter Balbina had a large goiter (a swelling in the neck resulting from an enlarged thyroid gland), and if Pope Alexander could heal her, then he would believe and become a Christian. Alexander told him to bring her to the prison where he was held originally.

"How can she find you there, when you're here with Hermes?" Quirinus asked. To which Pope Alexander replied, "He who brought me here, will also bring me back." So, Quirinus quickly returned home and brought his daughter to the prison where he had originally locked up Pope Alexander. There, to his amazement, he found Alexander patiently waiting for them, tightly shackled in the way he had been before. Seeing this, Quirinus and Balbina knelt before him in reverence.

Full of devotion, Balbina started to kiss the links of the chains to which the Pope was attached. But he said to her, "You should not kiss these chains – instead, go out and find Saint Peter's chains. Once you've found them, kiss them with devotion and you will soon be well."

Knowing where Peter had been held before his martyrdom, Quirinus jumped up immediately, took Balbina with him, went to the spot, and there they found the chains. Balbina kissed them as instructed, and was shortly cured of her illness. Overjoyed, Quirinus then pulled the necessary strings (the legal paperwork) to have Pope Alexander and governor Hermes pardoned and released. Shortly thereafter, Quirinus, his wife, and Balbina were baptized by the Pope. Alexander stipulated that the miracle of the chains should be celebrated in the church from that day forward.[2]

At some later time, Quirinus was arrested for being a Christian. He was martyred by decapitation in 116 AD, and buried in the catacombs on the Via Appia (The Appian Way). Balbina lived as a virgin recluse until 130 AD. In that year, she was also found guilty of being a Christian, and was sentenced to death under the emperor Hadrian. She was executed either by drowning or by being buried alive (a matter of some dispute among historians). After her death, she was buried next to her father in the catacombs.[3]

POTAMIAENA – ALEXANDRIA, EGYPT (~208 AD)

EARLY in the third century, during the persecutions under the emperor Septimus Severus, there was a very notable female martyr named Potamiaena, whose courage, faith, and prayers as she faced death, actually converted her jailer. Many stories are still celebrated today among the citizens of Alexandria about the innumerable tortures, dreadful and terrible, that she endured for her faith and for her virtue. For besides the perfections of her mind and her heart, she was also blooming in the maturity of personal attractions. Her fortitude in suffering for Christ became legend.

She and her mother Marcella were arrested in Alexandria, Egypt for refusing to revere the Roman gods. After suffering preliminary tortures aimed at exacting confessions, Potamiaena was threatened with being physically abused by gladiators, if she refused to renounce her Christianity. But she answered that only Christ was her king and her God. The judge regarded this response as impious and ordered her immediate death by fire, along with her mother.

After receiving the sentence of condemnation, Potamiaena was led away to die by an officer in the army named Basilides. When the crowd attempted to assault and insult her with abusive language in the corridor, Basilides intervened and protected her, restraining their insolence. In doing this, he exhibited the greatest compassion and kindness to her. Perceiving this man's sympathy and kindheartedness, Potamiaena encouraged him to be of good cheer, and promised him that in return for his kindness, she would not forget him with her Lord when she reached her destination – that after she was dead, she would reappear in a resurrected body, and intercede for him with the Lord.

After having said this, she was led into the arena for the torture and execution spectacle. Boiling pitch was poured over different parts of her body, little by little, from her feet up to the crown of her head. To the end, the noble Potamiaena endured the torture with poise, and never renounced her faith.

Not long after, being urged to swear to a pagan god by his fellow soldiers because of a slight indiscretion by them on a recent occasion that needed covering up (an alibi), Basilides declared that it was not proper for him to swear to the god, because he was a Christian. At first, they thought he was only joking, but as this behavior continued, and he persevered in the assertion that he was a Christian, they eventually denounced him, and he was brought before the local judge. But Basilides didn't waver – he again confessed his faith – and not surprisingly, was committed to prison for an eventual sentence of beheading.

When some of the covert local Christian believers (the famous Christian scholar Origen, possibly being one of them) came to see him and inquired into the cause of his sudden change of heart, he explained to them that Potamiaena had stood before him at night, every day for three days after her martyrdom. He told them that she placed a crown of flowers upon his head, as a pledge that the Lord would soon receive him into his glory, and said that she had prayed and pleaded to the Lord on his account. Furthermore, he said that she stated that the Lord had answered her prayer, and that very shortly she would take him with her to heaven.[4] Upon hearing this amazing account, the believers baptized him with water and the seal of the Lord.

The next day, he was brought again before the judge and given the opportunity to recant and profess the proper Roman religion. But Basilides adamantly refused, and instead gave a rousing and inspirational testimony for the Lord. That same day, he was summarily executed by beheading.

Six young Christians, students of the great scholar Origen,[5] were martyred at the same time. The first of these was named Plutarch. As he was being led to his death, another friend who promised to stick by him until the end, was almost killed by annoyed and enraged citizens who thought that he was trying to magically save the convicted man. But the providence of God preserved the samaritan. After Plutarch, the second martyr among the pupils of Origen was Serenus, who through the ordeal of fire, gave great proof of the faith which he had received. The third martyr from the same school was Heraclides, yet a catechumen, and after him the fourth was Hero, who had just recently been baptized. Both of them were summarily executed by beheading. After them, the fifth from the same school was another man of piety also named Serenus. He was also beheaded. But being in strong athletic health, it came about only after a long endurance of tortures. And there was one gallant woman with the group, the heroic Herais, who never wavered and died while still a catechumen, receiving baptism by fire.

The believers then disseminated this remarkable story to the whole of Alexandria, and many people of the city became introduced to the teachings of Christ, and many became converted. It is said that Potamiaena appeared in the dreams of many – pleading with them to accept the Good News of Jesus Christ and the future resurrection – and many became believers, embracing the divine Word of God.

CECILIA – ROME (~230 AD)

CECILIA was born to a Roman senatorial family and was baptized a Christian in infancy. Together with her husband Valerian, his brother Tiburtius, and a Roman soldier named Maximus, she suffered martyrdom under the reign of emperor Alexander Severus.

Despite her vow of virginity, Cecilia was forced by her parents to marry a pagan nobleman named Valerian. As the musicians played during their wedding, a despondent Cecilia sat alone and apart, singing in her heart to the Lord.[6] When the time came for the marriage to be consummated, Cecilia told Valerian that an angel of the Lord was watching over her and protecting her virginity – anyone who sexually violated her would be severely punished – and anyone who respected her virginity would be greatly loved.

"I have an angel that loves me, and keeps watch over my body whether I sleep or wake," she said. "If he finds that you have touched my body by villainy, or by foul or polluted love, then he will kill you straight away. However, if he finds that you love me in holy love and cleanness, then he will love you just as he loves me – and he will show you his grace."

Upon hearing this, Valerian asked whether he could see and talk to the angel. Then Cecilia replied, "If you will believe in Almighty God, and in Jesus Christ His only begotten Son, then you can be baptized in the 'Way'. If you do this, you will be able to see the angel. So, if you wish, go now to the Via Appia, which is about three miles out of town, and there you will find bishop Urban among the poor folks. Tell him these words that I have said to you. And if you are found worthy, then he will purge you from all sin by baptizing you. Then you can come to me again and you will see the angel."

Loving her with all of his heart, and not wanting to lose her, Valerian followed Cecilia's advice, and went to see bishop Urban. There he was taught about the way, the truth, and the life of Christ, and was baptized by the bishop.

When he returned home, he saw Cecilia conversing with an angel who was holding two crowns, one of roses and one of lilies. Acknowledging his presence, the angel placed the crown of lilies on his head and the crown of roses on Cecilia's head. The angel then asked Valerian if there was any one wish that he could fulfill. Jumping at this good fortune, Valerian asked only that his pagan brother Tiburtius be brought to know the joy of life in the 'Way'. And with that, the angel disappeared. The next day, Valerian and Tiburtius went to see bishop Urban, and Tiburtius was baptized shortly thereafter.

Cecilia welcomed Christians into her home, and it became a place of learning and worship. But persecution in Rome against Christians was getting worse. Good people were being rounded up and martyred, almost on a daily basis. Now, it was the custom – even the holy responsibility – of the believers to try as earnestly as possible to retrieve the body of a martyred Christian – often at great risk, in order to give it a proper Christian burial. Unfortunately, the Roman authorities were aware of the practice and were on the lookout for people trying to steal the remains of the bodies (they were even known to set traps with the intention of luring unsuspecting Christians sneaking around at night).

One night, Valerian and Tiburtius received word that the body of a recent Christian martyr was lying in a certain place.

So, they set out to try and retrieve the body before the authorities could burn it and scatter the ashes, or feed it to the wolves. They found the body as projected, but as they were about to wrap it and carry it back, they were surprised and intercepted by a Roman soldier named Maximus. He was a good and kind man, but he knew that these two men and this activity should be reported to the authorities. But Valerian explained to him the importance of burying the body in anticipation of the resurrection, which was to come soon. Together, the two brothers told him all about our Lord, our God, and our Way, and he listened intently. He wanted to know more and whether he could be baptized. So, the three of them talked and worked together to move the body of the martyr to a Christian burial site. But as they approached the site, they were apprehended by Roman police officers who had staked out the site, knowing that Christians could be coming there. The two brothers and the soldier were roughed up and whisked away to a holding prison.

The next day, the three were brought before the judge Turcius Almachius. The trial was quick, they were found guilty of crimes against the Roman people. They were beheaded that very evening.

Late that night, Cecilia tried to retrieve the bodies of her husband and his brother. But she too was apprehended in the same vile snare of wickedness, and hauled off to a holding cell.

The next day, she was brought before the same judge. Feeling somewhat sympathetic towards the young woman, he said that if she made a sacrifice to the gods, she could be freed with just a warning. But Cecilia outright refused the temptation, and was therefore condemned. The judge ordered a merciful sentence – suffocation in her own home. And that night, the executioner went to her house to carry out the sentence. But Cecilia would not die. No matter how constraining the pressure, Cecilia managed to get just enough breaths to survive.

On the following day, she was again brought before the judge and asked again to renounce her faith and her actions. But once again, Cecilia refused. So, she was immediately sent to the executioner for beheading.

However, the execution didn't quite go as planned. Even with three strikes on the neck with a sword, her head was not severed completely and she continued to live. Thinking that she was possessed by a god or a demon, the executioner refused further attempts. She was led back to prison, bleeding profusely.

But amazingly, Cecilia lived for three days with makeshift first-aid. During this time, she preached the Faith to many visitors, and sent many people to bishop Urban to be baptized. And she asked him to convert her home into a church.

Bishop Urban and his deacons buried her body in the catacomb of Callixtus, and hallowed her house. A few years later, she was transferred to the Church of Santa Cecilia in Trastevere, which was founded by now-Pope Urban I, and built on the very spot where her house once stood.

In 1599, her body was found still incorrupt, seeming to be asleep.[7]

AGATHA OF PALERMO – SICILY (~251 AD)

A heroic martyr of the third century, Agatha was born in Catania (or Palermo), Sicily, and martyred for her determined profession of faith at the age of 20, under the rule of emperor Decius. She is venerated as one of the 'celebrated Christian virgins and martyrs' in sixth century poetry.

Born in a rich and noble family, Agatha turned to Christianity and made a vow of virginity when 15 years old. Recognizing that this was unpopular at the time, she fled from Sicily and took refuge in Malta, together with some of her friends. There, she spent her days in a rock-hewn crypt at Rabat, praying and teaching the Christian Faith to children. But her stay on the island was short, and she soon returned to Sicily.

Back in Sicily, she became the subject of amorous advances by the Roman governor Quintianus, who thought he could force her to turn away from her vow and marry him. But his persistent proposals were consistently spurned by Agatha. Knowing that she was a Christian, Quintianus reported her to the legal authorities. He expected her to give in to his demands when she was faced with torture and possible death, but it wasn't to be – she simply reaffirmed her belief in God by praying,

Jesus Christ, Lord of all, you see my heart, you know my desires. Possess all that I am. I am your sheep. Make me worthy to overcome the devil.

With tears falling from her eyes, she prayed for courage. To coerce her into changing her mind, Quintianus sent Agatha to the keeper of a brothel, named Aphrodisia, and had her imprisoned there. But Agatha was not coerced and never lost her confidence in God.

After a time, Quintianus sent for her again. He argued, pleaded, and threatened, but nothing changed. Finally, he had her imprisoned and then tortured. She was stretched on a rack, slashed with iron hooks, burned with torches, and flogged with whips. Finally, she endured the torture of having her breasts cut off with rudimentary pincers. Even after all that, Agatha remained unrepentant. In fact, with exceptional fortitude and steadfast devotion, she dramatically engaged Quintianus in philosophical argument as he was making verbal assault on Christian logic. But it was to little avail –

Quintianus was beyond redemption. He ordered that she be burned at the stake immediately.

Under the protection of the holy angels, Agatha was saved by an earthquake that occurred just as she was about to be executed. The fire at the stake was extinguished and she was spared from the fate. Worried that she might be under the protection of one of the gods, Quintianus decided that sending her to prison was the safest thing to do. She remained there for about four years, out of sight and out of mind. It is said that she was visited by Saint Peter the Apostle, who tended to her wounds and gave her comfort. The heroic Agatha eventually died in prison.[8]

PRISCA – ROME (~269 AD)

A child martyr, Prisca died at the age of 13. She lived in Rome and her parents were from a noble Christian family. At the time, Claudius II was the emperor, and it was dangerous to be a Christian. During that time, it was not always best to say out loud exactly what one thought. Her father and mother went to church in secret chapels underground, and they were not suspected of being Christians.

But being young, naïve, and immature, Prisca believed in Jesus Christ and wasn't afraid to show it. Many people knew this, and eventually she was reported to the regional authorities. Being so young, she was bounced in and out of courts, never renouncing her faith. Until finally, she was taken by the guards and brought before the emperor. Claudius was surprised at how young she was and thought he could change her mind and make her obey him. He ordered his men to take her to one of the seven hills of Rome, and offer incense to the god of the silver bow. She was taken to the temple of Apollo, the sun-god, and was placed in front of a fire. They gave her incense and demanded that she throw it into the fire in honor of the sun-god. Prisca knew that it was wrong to worship false gods, and refused. Finding this out, the emperor became angry and told the soldiers to whip her until she obeyed. But she wouldn't obey – she remained resolute in her defiance. So, additional tortures were ordered.

They poured boiling tallow upon her and then whipped her some more.[9] But Prisca remained silent. Interestingly, the people of Rome admired her bravery, and thought it was cruel to treat a child like that. Nevertheless, in the middle of the whipping she began to glow in a robe of yellow sunshine. A glorious light shone around her, and she seemed to be a human star giving off light. The emperor did not understand how she could bear so much suffering. He didn't want to kill her – and face the wrath of the populace – but she wasn't cooperating. He had to take further action to force her to recant.

After the beating and torture, Prisca was placed in a dark dirty prison and kept cold and hungry for three days. At length, a guard came for her and brought her to the amphitheater, which was filled with people. She sat in the middle praying for courage as the door of a den was opened, and a great lion was let out. The lion let out a dreadful roar and ran towards Prisca, but it recognized a gentle soul and refused to attack her. Instead, it walked softly up to her and crouched down by her side. The whole place went silent, and the emperor watched as she stroked the lion's mane.

Obviously, more torture was needed. So, they took her and tied her upon the rack. Pieces of flesh were torn from her body with iron hooks, and then she was thrown on a burning pile. But throughout, Prisca remained alive and never renounced her faith.

Admiring her bravery, it was decided to give her one more chance to recant. So, Prisca was placed in the heathen temple and told to sacrifice to the gods, and give up the vile religion of Christianity, or else. By now Prisca was ill and tired, but still she would not give in. When the guards finally realized that she would not give up and obey, they brought her outside the Ostian gate to the tenth milestone post on the Via Ostiensis,[10] and waited for orders.

The orders came shortly. And so, the 13-year-old child Prisca was beheaded that day. She never cried or screamed or was even afraid. It is legend that when she died, an eagle hovered over her body – when the soldiers came near, the eagle swooped down with dreadful cries. No one dared to touch the body of Prisca because they were afraid of the great eagle. At night, the Christians secretly came to take the body for proper burial – and the eagle allowed them to take her. They buried her in a secret underground chamber (catacomb), one that would not be found by the authorities.[11]

At this time, few people in Rome dared to speak of God for fear of being persecuted, even the big and strong. But Prisca, frail and weak, was motivated to stay firm even when she saw everyone else around her becoming meek. She stood up for her beliefs and that resolve affected others. Many citizens of Rome saw her unshakable courage – how much she truly believed in her faith – and were moved.

KYRIAKI THE GREAT MARTYR – NICOMEDIA (286-293 AD)

A devout Christian couple of Greek heritage, but living in Nicomedia, were wealthy but childless. Unceasing in prayer, Dorotheus and Eusebia finally obtained a child, and since she was born on Sunday, the Lord's Day, she was given the name Kyriaki, the Greek word for Sunday.

From her childhood, Kyriaki consecrated herself to God. As she was a beautiful young woman, many suitors asked for her hand in marriage, but she refused them all saying that she wished to die as a virgin, since she had dedicated herself to Jesus Christ. It so happens that a magistrate of Nicomedia also wished to betroth Kyriaki to his son, especially since she came from a wealthy family. But when she once more rejected his proposal, he denounced Kyriaki and her parents as Christians to the authorities. The case eventually went to the co-emperor Diocletian.

The emperor ordered the family to be arrested, and upon their refusal to honor the pagan gods, Dorotheus was beaten until the soldiers grew tired and were unable to continue. Since the beating was unable to extract a confession, Dorotheus and Eusebia were exiled to Melitene in eastern Anatolia. But Kyriaki was separated and kept in Nicomedia to be interrogated by the co-emperor Maximian, who promised her great wealth if she worshiped the pagan gods and married one of Diocletian's relatives. When Kyriaki refused to renounce her faith, Maximian ordered that she be whipped and flogged. Interestingly, the soldiers who were assigned the punishment task had to be replaced three times, as they became tired from the exertion.

Since Maximian had failed to persuade the young woman to change her faith, he sent her to Hilarion, the mayor of Bithynia in Chalcedon, with an ultimatum: either convert Kyriaki to paganism, or send her back to him (with unspecified consequences). Hilarion tried his best to achieve the goal, including using promises and threats, but when all of these proved ineffective, he ordered her tortured. So, she was then suspended by her hair for several hours, while soldiers burned her body with torches. Finally, she was taken down and thrown into a prison cell.

During the night, an angel appeared to her and healed her wounds. Seeing the miraculous recovery of Kyriaki, many pagans converted to Christianity, but once found out by the authorities, they were all beheaded. The next day, Hilarion announced that the gods had healed her out of pity – and commanded her to go to the temple in order to give them thanks. When she was brought to the pagan temple, Kyriaki prayed that God would destroy the idols. And suddenly, a fierce storm and earthquake occurred, toppling all the idols, and shattering them to pieces. Upon seeing what happened, Hilarion cursed the god of the Christians. But with that, he was struck by lightning and died on the spot.

The successor to Hilarion was a man named Apollonius. He was even more ruthless and determined to see Kyriaki properly punished. So, once again she was subjected to torture. First, she was thrown into a fire pit, but the flames became extinguished. Then, she was thrown into the arena with wild beasts, but they became gentle and docile. Exasperated that the torture was ineffective, Apollonius then sentenced her to death by the sword.

Kyriaki was given very little time to pray, but in the few moments available to her, she asked Almighty God to receive her soul and to remember those who honored her martyrdom. Upon completing her prayer, she rendered her soul to God just seconds before the sword was lowered on her neck.

Pious Christians took her relics and buried them before they could be desecrated by the authorities. At the time of her death, the saintly martyr Kyriaki was 21 years old.

THE GREAT MARTYR BARBARA – NICOMEDIA (286-305 AD)
(also known as Barbara and the Tower)

Daughter of a rich pagan named Dioscorus in Heliopolis, Phoenicia (present-day Baalbek, Lebanon), Barbara was carefully guarded by her father to protect her from the outside world. Once a teenager, he arranged a marriage for her with a local pagan, but she disliked the man and rejected the offer. To protect her against the suitor's retribution, he kept her locked up in a tower. During this time, Barbara decided to accept Christianity.

Shortly afterwards, before going on a journey, the father commissioned a new bath-house with two windows to be built next to the tower for her personal use. However, during his absence, Barbara had three windows installed, as a symbol of the Holy Trinity. When her father returned and asked about the extra window, she acknowledged herself to be a Christian. Upon hearing this sacrilege, he drew his sword with intent to kill her, but she prayed to God and an opening miraculously appeared in the tower wall, whereby she escaped unharmed.

She ran off into the mountains and found a hiding place near where two shepherds were tending their flocks. She asked them not to reveal her place to her pursuing father, and they agreed. When Dioscorus arrived, he was rebuffed by the first shepherd, but the second shepherd betrayed her. For doing this, legend has it that he was turned to stone and his flock was changed to locusts.

Barbara was captured and dragged back to the tower, but still confessed to being a Christian. Consequently, her father had her brought before the judge of the province, Martinianus, who found her twice guilty – not obeying her father and confessing to be a Christian. For this, she was cruelly tortured with various implements for many days. But throughout, Barbara held true to her Christian faith.

At some point during every night, the dark prison would be bathed in light, and wondrous miracles would occur. Every morning, her day's wounds would be healed. And torches that were meant to be used to burn her, mysteriously went out as soon as they came near her.

Finally, she was condemned to death by beheading. Her wicked father himself carried out the execution. However, as punishment, legend has it that he was struck by lightning on the way home, and his body was consumed by flame. Barbara was buried by a friendly Christian in a Christian grave, and her tomb became the site of many miracles.[12]

CHRISTINA OF BOLSENA – ITALY (~300 AD)
(also known as Christina of Tyre; Christina the Great Martyr)

BORN in Tuscany, Lebanon, or Persia, Christina was brought up in a rich family, her father Urbain (or Urbanus, Urban) being a powerful magistrate (combination governor and judge). He was deep into the practices of heathenism and kept a large number of golden idols. He was solidly patriotic to the empire and deeply attached to the assorted Roman deities.

By the age of 11, Christina was exceptionally beautiful, and many wealthy men wanted to marry her. However, her father envisioned that his daughter should become a pagan priestess. To this end he placed her in a special room where he had set up many gold and silver idols – and he commanded his daughter to burn incense before them. She even had two servants attending her.

Christina often peered at the world outside her window and decided there must have been a great creator of the world. Looking at the idols, she came to believe that they could not possibly represent the creators of the world. So, she began to pray to the true creator of the world and asked him to reveal himself to her by a sign. That was when she began to feel an intense love blaze from deep within her heart. She began to fast and continued to pray.

Her father was an enemy to the Christians, and hardly a day passed when he did not call one of them into his presence and doom them to suffering or death. Christina was very young, but on seeing this, she was struck by how fearless and happy the Christians were during their torments. She was curious to know what kind of people these were, why they were persecuted and what gave them the strength to bear the sufferings they endured. So, she sought out someone who could teach her about the Christian faith, secretly called him in, and in short order she was baptized as a Christian without her parents' knowledge.

Then one night, she was visited by an angel, who instructed her fully in the Gospel of Christ – the true faith – and how the world was created. He called her a 'bride of Christ', but warned that she would suffer for her faith.

The next day, with renewed vigor and enlightenment, Christina smashed all the false idols and threw them out through the window (where the street urchins gratefully grabbed them for the monetary value). When her father came to visit later that day and discovered the missing idols, he questioned her about it, but she wouldn't give a good answer. However, after summoning the servants, he learned the truth from them about everything – the idols and Christina's new religion.

Urbain was furious and resolved to avenge the dishonor done to the gods with his daughter's blood. Enraged, he began to slap his daughter's face, demanding that she renounce this vile religion of the Christians and pay proper homage to the Roman gods. But Christina refused, saying:

Do with me whatever you like, my dear father; you can take my life, but you have no power to tear the faith of Christ out of my heart. My Savior will strengthen me to suffer patiently all that you have threatened.

And thus, her father ordered her to be beaten – but she gave no signs of pain in her suffering. Again he had her beaten, and again Christina looked to heaven and thanked Almighty God for aiding her to bear her pain. Her father then ordered that she be tied to an iron wheel. A fire was lit beneath it to burn the girl. But she sang a song of praise all the while, remaining unhurt by the flames. Exasperated, her father threw her into a dungeon so as to begin again the next day. Her mother came and pleaded with her to renounce her faith, but Christina politely refused, her mother throwing up her hands in exasperation and leaving her to the will of the gods.

That night in the dungeon, an angel appeared to her and healed her wounds. The angel encouraged her to persevere and gave her assurance of divine assistance.

When her father heard of this healing the next day, he had her brought into court for official trial and judging. She was ordered to worship the pagan gods and to beg for forgiveness with a sacrifice – or else. But Christina refused all orders, holding fast to her new Christian faith and never wavering. The order for execution was then delivered.

An executioner was commanded to tie a large stone around her neck and cast her deep into the lake. But the angel who had visited her the day before, untied the stone, sustained her, and carried her safely to shore. When she reappeared unhurt above the water, Urbain was exceedingly irritated and angry. He attributed her survival to sorcery – the Christians must have turned her into a witch! So, he had her sent back to the dungeon while he pondered what to do next. But that night her father died – he was found dead the next morning. It is presumed he died from a stroke, or apoplexy brought on by his uncontrolled anger and vexation.

Within a few days, a new regional governor arrived to continue with Christina's punishment and execution, in her father's stead. His name was Dio, and he was even more cruel towards the Christians than Urbain. He ordered an iron cradle to be built and filled with boiling oil and tar. Christina was summoned and tortured by immersing her in the cradle. However, she made the 'sign of the cross' and said to the soldiers, "It is fitting that you lay me like a child in a cradle, for it is hardly a year since I was born again in holy baptism." Throughout the ensuing ordeal, she was not harmed and experienced no pain.

Dio then had Christina taken to the temple of Apollo. She was ordered to make fitting sacrifice to Apollo, so as to please the god and preclude any retribution on the community. But when she stepped into the temple and made the 'sign of the cross', the image of Apollo immediately fell from the altar and was broken into a thousand pieces. The soldiers who brought her to the temple were terrified, and quickly released her exclaiming, "Truly the god of Christina and the Christians is the one true God!" Many of those who witnessed this event were converted. But the unconvinced pagan soldiers brought her back to the prison, where she languished for another week.

Julian succeeded Dio as governor, and he was even more ruthless. He gave Christina a final choice: sacrifice to the gods or be thrown into a fiery furnace. But she would not be tempted and continued to profess her faith. And with that, she was thrown into the furnace, where she remained for five days. But much like the companions of Daniel during their exile in Babylon,[13] Christina remained unharmed and unshaken.

Not giving up, Julian had Christina thrown into a cavern where there were many vicious animals. Again, she made the 'sign of the cross' and none of the wild animals would touch her. All the while, she sang praises to God, and the animals listened. Tired of her singing, the guards tore out her tongue with knives. But she continued to pray silently and the animals were held at bay.

Finally, she was tied to a pole and shot with a flurry of arrows. And just to make sure that she was really dead, she was stabbed with a sword. With that, the heroic Christina gave up the ghost and went to heaven to meet her Maker.

During her time in captivity, it is said that she converted nearly 300 people.

DEMIANA AND THE 40 VIRGINS – EGYPT (~302 AD)
(also known as the Chaste Martyr Demiana)

NEAR the end of the third century, there lived a Christian named Mark. He was the governor of the el-Borollos, el-Zaafaran, and Wadi al-Saysaban districts in the northern delta of the Nile River in Egypt. Mark had an only-child named Demiana, who he loved dearly. When Demiana was still very young, her mother died, and her father did his utmost to raise her as a virtuous Christian.

When she was 15, her father wanted her to marry one of his noble friends, but she politely refused. She said she had devoted herself as a bride of Christ and intended to live in celibacy and serve the Lord. Demiana requested that her father build her an isolated house on the outskirts of the city, where she could live with her pious friends, away from the world and its temptations.

So, Mark granted her wish and built her a large palace-like manor in the wilderness. Demiana changed the manor into a monastery for nuns,[14] living the monastic, ascetic life with her 40 unmarried friends. Demiana was the abbess, and the nuns spent their time fasting, praying, reading the holy scriptures, and providing for themselves and the poor by means of their handiwork.

At that time, the pagan emperor Diocletian began to torture and kill Christians who refused to worship the gods and idols of Rome (especially Apollo and Artemis). When Mark was ordered to kneel before the idols and offer incense, he initially refused. However, after some not-so-friendly persuasion, he relented and venerated the idols. When news reached Demiana that her father had knelt down and offered incense in worship to the idols, she reproached him severely. Mark was emotionally moved by her words, and bitterly repented.

Thinking that he had to address the emperor directly about this policy, Mark traveled to Antioch, where Diocletian was currently staying. Without second thought, he made the 'sign of the cross' in front of the emperor, nobles, princes, soldiers, and all the people attending, proudly declaring himself to be a Christian. But this tactic did not go over well. The emperor was furious and said, "I have tried to keep our friendship, but now you insult me in front of all. If you do not carefully reconsider your words, your days are ended". But Mark refused to reconsider and remained silent. With that, the emperor ordered Mark to be beheaded by the sword. And within the hour, Mark was dead.

When the emperor learned that it was Mark's daughter, Demiana, who had persuaded her father to return to the abominable religion of the Christians, and behave so disrespectfully in front of the court, he ordered one of his commanders to confront her manor with 100 soldiers. The order was this: "First, try to convince her to worship our idols by offering her riches and glory, but if she refuses, then threaten her, torture her, and even behead her and her followers, to make them an example to all the other despicable Christians."

Demiana saw the soldiers approaching, and prayed to God to strengthen her faith and the faith of the nuns. She told her 40 friends: "If you are willing to die for Jesus' sake then you may stay, but if you cannot withstand the torments of the soldiers, then hurry and escape now." All 40 of the women replied, "We will die with you."

The commander relayed the emperor's message to Demiana by saying: "I am an envoy sent by emperor Diocletian. By his orders, I command you to worship the gods, so that he may grant you whatsoever you wish." To which Demiana shouted in reply:

Cursed be the messenger and he who sent him. There is no other god in heaven or on earth besides the one and only True God – the Father, the Son, and the Holy Spirit – the Creator, who has no beginning and no end – the omnipresent and omniscient God who will throw you in hell for eternal condemnation. As for me, I worship my Lord and Savior Jesus Christ, His Good and Holy Father, and the Holy Spirit. I profess the Trinity of Perfection – and in His name I will die, and by Him I will live forever.

The commander was enraged, and ordered her to be placed in the squeezing press until blood poured on the ground. Severely wounded, she was thrown in prison. But an angel of the Lord appeared to her, touched her body with his illumined wings, and she was healed of all her wounds. In the following days, she was subjected to additional tortures, but through it all her faith sustained her, and her resolve never faltered.

Finally, the commander issued an order for Demiana and the 40 followers to be beheaded. The bloody order was carried out without fanfare, and they all received three heavenly crowns – for purity, endurance of torture, and righteous martyrdom.[15]

PHILOMENA – ROME (~304 AD)

THE story of Philomena is mostly based on the accounts of Sister Maria Luisa di Gesù (1799–1875), a Dominican nun from Naples, who claimed to have received revelations from Philomena herself. The name (Filumena) is thought to mean 'daughter of light' and derived from a Greek word meaning 'beloved'.

According to the nun's account, Philomena was the daughter of a local ruler in Greece who, with his wife, had converted to Christianity. At the age of about 13, she took a vow of consecrated virginity. When the emperor threatened to pacify the area militarily (possibly because of Christian disturbances), her father went to Rome to negotiate for peace, and took the family with him. Once there, the emperor became enamored with the young Philomena, and claiming that he was in love with her, asked for her hand in marriage.[16] The parents advised her to consent (to avoid all sorts of repercussions), but she adamantly refused, and they respected her wishes.

Of course, the emperor did not take rejection kindly. Neither threats of pain or promises of wealth could change the mind of Philomena. Consequently, she was subjected to a series of torments as punishment for disobedience. First, she was scourged with a whip, but the story is that two angels appeared that night and smoothed her wounds. Then she was thrown into the river with an anchor attached to her feet, but the story is that the two angels came and cut the rope, raising her to the river bank. Next, she was shot with arrows three times. On the first occasion, the story is that her wounds were healed by the angels; on the second occasion, the story is that the arrows turned aside; and on the third occasion, the story is that the arrows turned around and killed six of the archers (seeing this, several of the others confessed and became Christians). Finally, the emperor ordered that she be beheaded by the sword, and this was carried out forthright.

In 1802, in the catacombs of Priscilla on the Via Salaria Nova, in Rome, an unusual space was found hollowed out of the rock. The space was covered with three terracotta tiles, on which was the inscription 'lumena paxte cumfi'. It was thought at the time that the tiles had not been positioned in the correct sequence, and that the inscription originally read, 'pax tecum Filumena' ('Peace with you, Philomena'). Within the space was found the skeleton of a female between 13 and 15 years old. Embedded in the cement was a small glass vial with traces of what appeared to be blood. In accordance with the protocols of the time, the remains were accepted as being those of a virgin martyr named Philomena. The symbolic designs on the tiles, showing anchors, arrows, and palm leaves, were interpreted as evidence of her martyrdom.[17]

LUCY OF SYRACUSE – ITALY (~304 AD)

WITH a Roman father and a Greek mother, Lucy was born to nobility and was strikingly beautiful. However, her father died when she was five years old, leaving Lucy and her mother Eutychia without a protective guardian. Like many of the early martyrs, Lucy had consecrated her virginity to God, and she hoped to distribute her inheritance to the poor. However, not knowing of Lucy's intention, and suffering from a bleeding disorder, Eutychia feared for her and Lucy's future. So, she arranged a marriage for Lucy to a young man of a wealthy pagan family.

52 years earlier, Saint Agatha had been martyred during the persecution of emperor Decius. Her shrine at Catania, less than 50 miles from Syracuse, attracted a large number of pilgrims, since many miracles were reported to have happened through her intercessions. Eutychia was persuaded to make a pilgrimage to Catania together with Lucy, in hopes of receiving a cure. While at the shrine, Saint Agatha came to Lucy in a dream and told her that because of her faith, her mother would be cured – and that Lucy would become the shining light of Syracuse, just as she had become the shining light of Catania.

Of course, the prediction miraculously occurred – and with her mother cured, Lucy took the opportunity to persuade her to allow an even greater part of her inheritance to be distributed among the poor. But Eutychia suggested that the money would be better spent as a bequest in a will. To this, Lucy countered,

...whatever you give away at death for the Lord's sake, you give because you cannot take it with you. Instead, whatever you intended to give away at your death, you should give now to the true Savior while you are still healthy.

Although initially unhappy with her decision to remain unwed, her mother permitted Lucy to live the life of poverty and celibacy that she so earnestly desired, and she became a supporter of the new faith.

Unfortunately, Lucy had been betrothed to a greedy and despicable young man who was jealous of her holiness. When news came to his attention that her endowment was being distributed to the poor, he chastised her and threatened retribution. He believed that it should instead have been given to him as the future bridegroom. But Lucy was unmoved. Enraged, he tried to force her into prostitution as punishment. She was dragged to a nearby brothel (the common penalty for women who refused to wed), but Lucy's resolve and determination were so strong that bringing her to that place was useless. No one could touch her or even come close to her. It was as if she was protected by an unseen force-field.

Angry that this punishment had no effect, the shameful fiancé denounced her to the authorities. Paschasius, the governor of Syracuse, was unsympathetic to her situation and ordered her to burn a sacrifice to the emperor's image. Of course, Lucy refused as this went against her Christian beliefs. The governor then sentenced her to be defiled in a brothel, this time under police custody. But when the guards came to take her away, they could not physically force her to move, even when they hitched her up to a team of oxen. Again, it was as if she was protected by an unseen force-field.

Finally, Paschasius ordered that she be burned at the stake. Bundles of wood were heaped about her and set on fire, but the fire refused to envelop her body and she remained unharmed. Once again, she seemed to be protected by an invisible force-field. At length, the executioners were compelled to kill her by the sword – thrust harshly into her throat – which granted Lucy her wish of perpetual virginity and sainthood.

Legend has it that Lucy was also tortured by eye-gouging. Before she died, she shouted predictions that Paschasius would be punished, the state persecution of Christians would end soon, the reign of emperor Diocletion would end very shortly, and that the junior-emperor Maximian would meet his end quickly. This so angered Paschasius that he ordered the guards to remove her eyes.[18] However, when her body was prepared for burial in the family mausoleum, it was discovered that her eyes had been miraculously restored.

Lucy's name means 'light', and she has been associated with the one true Light who came into the world to cast out all darkness.[19]

AGNES OF ROME – ITALY (~304 AD)

AGNES, another young woman, was martyred in the same year as Lucy, but in Rome. Although barely 13 years old, she faced death with an extraordinary courage and maturity. She spurned would-be suitors since she had already consecrated her chastity and dedicated her life completely to Christ. Unsurprisingly, one of the rejected then brought official charges against her of being a Christian – a serious offense. However, she preferred death of body in preference to desecration of her virginity by an unbeliever. This child-martyr has been honored for suffering the tortures so bravely in such a small body:

There was not even room in her little body for a wound. Though she could barely receive the sword's point, she overcame it. Nowadays, girls of her age tend to wilt under the slightest frown from a parent – pricked by a needle, they cry as if given a mortal wound. But Agnes showed no fear of the blood-stained hands of her executioners. She was undaunted by the weight of clanging chains. She offered her whole body to the sword of the menacing soldiers.

Too young to have any real comprehension of death, she nevertheless stood ready before it. Dragged against her will to the pedestal of sacrifice (the burning stake), she stretched out her hands to Christ in the midst of the flames, making the triumphant sign of Christ the Victor (the sign of the cross), and she was not harmed. She was then prepared to put her neck and hands into iron bands – though none of them were small enough to enclose her tiny limbs. So, she stood still, praying, and offered up her neck. At the sight of this, the executioner began to tremble, as though he were himself condemned. Aware of her danger and predicament, his right hand began to shake violently, and his face drained of all color, though the child herself showed no fear.

Agnes courageously chose to retain her innocence and purity of heart all the way to her death – out of love for God she gained a martyr's crown.

VICTORIA, RESTITUTA, AND THE MARTYRS OF ABITINAE – NORTH AFRICA (~304 AD)

BOTH Victoria and Restituta were from North African noble families, who had refused arranged marriages because of their Christian leanings. On her wedding day, Victoria leaped from a window in her parents' house and ran away. But she was quickly apprehended and arrested. Victoria argued with the judge at her trial, who was willing to release her, but the prosecutors stood firm, arguing that she was a

Christian. She was then shepherded in with a bunch of other Christians that had been just recently rounded up.

The Martyrs of Abitinae were a group of 49 Christians (including about 20 women, 4 children, and 1 infant) found guilty during the reign of emperor Diocletian, of having illegally celebrated Sunday worship at Abitinae, a town in the Roman province of Africa.[20] The year before, an edict had been published that ordered the destruction of Christian scriptures and places of worship across the empire, and prohibiting Christians from assembling for worship.

The local bishop in Abitinae, Fundanus, obeyed the edict and handed the scriptures of the church over to the authorities, but some of the Christians continued to meet secretly with the priest Saturninus. They were eventually found out, arrested, and brought before the local magistrate, who sent them to Carthage, the capital of the province, for trial.

The trial took place before the judge Anullinus. One of the group was named Dativus, a senator. During his interrogation, he declared that he was a Christian, and had taken part in the meeting of the Christians, but even under duress he refused to say who presided over it. However, during the questioning, the prosecutor Fortunatianus, a brother of Victoria, denounced Dativus of having enticed her and other naïve young girls into attending the meeting. Victoria maintained that she had gone entirely of her own accord, but her statement was declared coerced. Interrupting the proceedings, the proconsul again asked Dativus (knowing that he now had damning evidence against him) whether he had taken part in the meeting. Dativus again declared that he had. Then, when asked who was the instigator, he reluctantly replied: "The priest Saturninus and all of us." He was then thrown into a prison.

The priest Saturninus was then interrogated, followed by all the members of the group. They all said the same thing: that they willfully wanted to go to the meeting on Sunday because it was absolutely mandatory per their religious beliefs – they couldn't imagine missing the experience because it meant peril to their immortal souls.

All the group members were then tortured in one way or another in an attempt to get them to beg for mercy and renounce their faith, but none of them ever changed their confession. In the end, the final verdict was death by torture. And the gruesome sentence was subsequently carried out on all of the group, men and women, and even on Saturninus' four children.

Somehow, Restituta survived her horrible torture. To quietly get rid of her, the soldiers placed her in a makeshift boat loaded with tree sap and resin, set it ablaze, and pushed it out to sea. But Restituta was unharmed by the fire, and prayed to God for her soul, and to forgive the persecutors. Hearing her supplication, God sent an angel to guide her boat to the island of Ischia, not far from Naples, and she landed at the present-day site of San Montano. But she had died on the journey from her wounds and malnutrition. Some local Christians found her in the wrecked boat beached on the shore, and gave her a proper burial at the foot of Monte Vico in Lacco Ameno.[21]

MARGARET OF ANTIOCH – SYRIA (~304 AD)
(also known as Margaret and the Dragon; Saint Margaret the Virgin; Saint Marina the Great Martyr)

A native of Antioch and the daughter of a pagan priest named Aedesius, Margaret's mother died soon after her birth, and she was raised by a Christian nurse a few miles outside the city. Having embraced Christianity and consecrated her virginity to God, Margaret was disowned by her father, adopted by her nurse, and lived in the country, keeping sheep with her foster mother. The governor of the Roman Diocese of the East, Olybrius, asked to marry her, but with the demand that she renounce Christianity. Upon her refusal, she was cruelly tortured – but legend has it that various miraculous incidents occurred during the terror. One of these involved being swallowed by a dragon (who was Satan in disguise), from which she escaped alive when the cross she carried irritated the dragon's inner organs.

Margaret is reputed to have promised very powerful indulgences to those who wrote or read about her life, or those who invoked her intercessions. This no doubt helped the spread of her notoriety. Margaret is one of the saints that Joan of Arc claimed to have spoken with.[22]

CATHERINE OF ALEXANDRIA – EGYPT (~305 AD)
(also known as Saint Catherine of the Wheel; The Great Martyr Saint Catherine; Holy Catherine the Great Martyr)

CATHERINE was both a princess and a noted scholar who became a Christian around the age of 14, converted hundreds of people to Christianity, and was martyred around the age of 18.[23] More than 1,100 years after Catherine's martyrdom, Joan of Arc identified her as one of the saints who appeared to her and gave her counsel.[24]

Catherine was the daughter of Constus, the governor of Alexandria during the reign of the western Roman emperor Maximian (286–305). From a young age she devoted herself to study. One day, a vision of the Virgin Mary and the Child Jesus persuaded her to become a Christian. When the persecutions began under the western junior-emperor Maxentius, she went personally to his court and rebuked him for his cruelty. The emperor summoned 50 of his best pagan philosophers and orators to dispute her with learned argument, hoping that they would be able to refute her pro-Christian stand. But they were no match for Catherine. She won the debate, easily outmaneuvering her opponents. Several of her adversaries, overwhelmed by her eloquence, declared themselves to be Christians – unfortunately, they were shortly afterwards put to death for this.[25]

Catherine was then imprisoned and scourged so severely that her whole body was covered with wounds, from which the blood flowed in streams. The spectators wept with pity, but Catherine stood with her eyes raised to heaven, without giving a sign of suffering or fear. Maxentius then ordered her to be incarcerated without food, so that she would starve into submission. However, legend has it that during the confinement, angels tended to her wounds with calming salve, and she was fed daily by a dove from Heaven. The spirit of Jesus Christ also appeared to her, encouraging her to fight bravely, and promised her the crown of everlasting glory.

During her imprisonment, more than 200 people came to see her, including Maxentius' wife Valeria Maximilla – all were converted to Christianity by her wisdom and grace – and all were subsequently martyred for it. Twelve days later, when the dungeon doors were opened, a bright light and fragrant perfume filled the air, and Catherine came forth even more radiant and beautiful than ever.

Upon failing to make Catherine yield by way of torture, Maxentius tried to win over the beautiful and wise princess by proposing that she become his mistress. Catherine staunchly refused, declaring that her spouse was Jesus Christ, to whom she had consecrated her virginity. The furious Maxentius then condemned Catherine to death on the spiked breaking wheel,[26] but at her touch, it cracked and then shattered. Finally, he ordered her to be executed by beheading.[27] Standing up proudly and showing no fear, Catherine herself ordered the execution to commence. At the dire moment, it is said that a milk-like substance flowed from her neck rather than blood. But Catherine's earthly life was ended.[28]

EUPHEMIA OF CHALCEDON – TURKEY (~307 AD)
(also known as Euphemia the All-Praised)

DURING the great persecutions under Roman emperor Diocletian, governor Priscur of Chalcedon,[29] a town located across the Bosporus from the city of Byzantium (modern-day Istanbul), issued a decree that all the inhabitants of the city must take part in sacrifices to the deity Ares.[30] Because of the cruelty of a local snitch, a young girl named Euphemia, daughter of a Roman senator and consecrated to chastity from her youth, was discovered with 49 other Christians hiding in a vacant house and worshipping God, in defiance of the governor's orders. Because of their refusal to sacrifice to the emperor, they were tortured for a number of days, and then, all but Euphemia, were sent to the governor for trial and possible execution.

Euphemia, the youngest, was separated from her companions and subjected to particularly harsh tortures, including the 'breaking wheel',[31] in hopes of breaking her will – but her spirit could not be broken. Later, she was placed in the public arena of Chalcedon, where lions were let out to kill her, but they instead licked her cuts and broken bones. Unfortunately, she died of wounds sustained from a subsequent attack by wild bears in the arena. However, she never renounced her faith and remained stoic throughout.

MENODORA, METRODORA, AND NYMPHODORA –
BITHYNIA (~308 AD)

DESPITE societal pressures, the three sisters from Bithynia in Asia Minor,[32] Menodora, Metrodora, and Nymphodora, chose not to marry, and to forsake the world. They found a home in a remote location outside the city and spent their days in fasting, prayer, and helping the poor and ailing. Many sick people from the city came to them for comfort, blessings, and healing.

When reports reached the governor of the region, Frontonius, that the sick were being miraculously healed as a result of the prayers of Christians, he ordered that they be arrested and brought before him. He had to learn whether they were witches, servants of the gods, charlatans, or demons.

At first, he tried to persuade them to renounce their faith, promising great honors and rewards. But the holy sisters steadfastly confessed their faith before him, rejecting all his offers and promises. They told him that they did not value the temporal things of this world, and that they were prepared to die for their heavenly bridegroom, since death would be their gateway to eternal life.

Of course, that just made the governor angry. Taking out his wrath on Menodora, the oldest sister, he had her stripped of her clothes and beaten by four men, while a deputy urged her to offer sacrifice to the gods. But she brave sister endured the torments and cried out, "Sacrifice? Don't you understand that I am already offering myself as a sacrifice to my God?" This meant nothing to the tormentors, and so they renewed their beatings with even greater severity. The cycle continued – torture followed by sacrificial request – followed by more torture. Finally, Menodora cried out, "Lord Jesus Christ, joy of my heart, my love and my hope, receive my soul in peace." And with these words, she gave up her soul to God, and went to be with her heavenly bridegroom.

Four days later, the two younger sisters Metrodora and Nymphodora were brought into the court. They were shown the battered body of their older sister, both to frighten them and shock them into renouncing their faith. The two women wept freely and profusely, but remained steadfast in their statements. So, Metrodora was tortured next, in a similar way as her older sister. And like her sister, she remained true to her faith to the end. As the torture became unbearable, she cried out with her last breath, "Lord Jesus Christ, my joy and my hope, receive my soul." And then she too, went to be with her Maker.

The persecutors then turned to the third sister, Nymphodora. Before her lay the bruised and lifeless bodies of her two sisters. Frontonius hoped that this horrendous sight would intimidate the young girl, and compel her to recant. Pretending that he was charmed by her youth and beauty, the governor implored her to worship the pagan gods, promising her great gifts and incentives. But Nymphodora scoffed at his words, saying, "I am already the bride of my Lord Jesus Christ." As payback for her impertinence, Frontonius had her tortured and beaten with iron rods. But she never relented. In the end, Nymphodora succumbed to the tormentors like her sisters before her.

The bodies of the holy martyrs were to be burned in a fire pit, but a heavy thunderstorm extinguished the flames. At nightfall, local Christians took the bodies of the holy sisters and reverently buried them in a Christian cemetery. It is said that lightning from the thunderstorm struck down governor Frontonius and his servant that very night.[33]

HOLY MARTYR VASILISSA – NICOMEDIA (~309 AD)

A small nine-year-old child when martyred, Vasilissa suffered in Nicomedia not long after the death of bishop Anthimus.[34] She is one of the many Christians who were martyred between 303 and 309 AD, in and around the city of Nicomedia, and collectively known as the '10,000 Martyrs of Nicomedia'.[35]

Vasilissa was accused of being a Christian and brought before the governor, a man named Alexander. She willingly acknowledged her faith, boldly responding that she was a pious Christian. For this, she was struck in the face – but undaunted, she just repeated that she was a pious Christian.

To induce her into giving up speaking such foolish nonsense, she was stripped naked and beaten with iron rods. But Vasilissa just continued to give praise to God. The governor grew tired and angry, so he ordered that she be laid out on the ground and whipped until her entire body became bruised and swollen. Enduring such torment, she was heard to say, "My God, I thank you for your love and mercy."

Still not satisfied with her response, he ordered that her ankles be pierced, and an iron hook be run through them. From the hook, a chain was tied, and from the chain Vasilissa was hung upside down. Beneath the child there was a fire of boiling pitch, lead, and sulfur, billowing dirty smoke into the air. She was positioned so that she was forced to breath in the smoke, the idea being that she would slowly suffer from asphyxiation until she either died, or relented and renounced her faith. But Vasilissa endured the torment, praising God all the while – it was almost as if she was relishing peace in paradise.

Alexander decided that a different approach was necessary. So, he ordered a furnace be lit, and that she be thrown into it. Just before being pushed into the furnace, Vasilissa sealed herself with the 'sign of the cross'. She was left in the furnace for a long time – long enough to turn a body to ashes – but amazingly she was unscathed. Everyone was astounded at this miracle, but the governor was still unconvinced and hard-hearted. So, he ordered that she be put to the wild beasts. But Vasilissa fell to her knees and prayed to God – and the beasts refused to attack her.

Finally, after seeing all these miraculous events, and witnessing the bravery of this little girl despite the deterioration and ruin of her body, Alexander's heart and soul became changed. He fell at the feet of the child, saying, "Have mercy on me, servant of the heavenly King, and forgive me for your torments that I brought upon you. Make me also a soldier of your King, because, as you have said, he accepts sinners like me." Then, thanking Almighty God, Vasilissa blessed the governor and asked that he be forgiven. She led him to bishop Anthimus, who baptized him into the church.

After receiving the sacrament of baptism, governor Alexander again fell down before Vasilissa, begging her again for a final forgiveness, saying, "Servant of the one true God, pray for me, that I may be forgiven of the evil sins that I did commit against you, and that my life will end with a good confession of faith." With that, the child Vasilissa prayed to God for his soul – and her prayers were heard by God – Alexander's earthly life was over. He gave up his soul while glorifying and blessing God. His body was consecrated by bishop Anthimus, and buried by the bishop and the holy young child.

Vasilissa's entire body was covered with wounds and injuries, but she remained faithful to Jesus Christ, and forgave her tormentors. Using all the strength she could muster, she limped into a field outside the city, and stood upon a large flat rock, praying to God. And at that moment, miraculously, a stream of crystal-clear water gushed out of the rock. Recognizing that this was a sign from God, she fell down to her knees in prayer, thanking God for His mercy and her endurance under torture. After drinking from the water, she staggered a few paces further and then collapsed to the ground. She could go on no more. She had fought the good fight and kept her faith. But her body was broken. Her last words were, "Lord, receive my spirit in peace." And with those words, she went to the Lord with joy and thanksgiving.

When bishop Anthimus heard about this, he hurried to the spot and made sure that she was given a proper Christian burial – near the rock from which gushed forth the crystal-clear water through the prayers of the child martyr. It is said that the water continues to flow even today.

NOTES

1. Pope Alexander I was the Bishop of Rome from roughly 107 to his death in 115 AD (some sources say 119 AD). He played an important part in the early development of the Church of Rome's emerging liturgical and administrative traditions.

2. To that end, the church of the Apostle Peter was built, where the chains have been held ever since. Today, the church is called 'Saint Peter in Chains'.

3. In the 4th century, a basilica devoted to Saint Balbina, was built on Aventine Hill over the house of a pagan politician, and the bones and relics of Quirinus and Balbina were brought to the church. Most of Balbina's relics are still in the altar. However, some of her relics were brought to Cologne Cathedral during the Middle Ages. And at some point in the late 15th or early 16th century, Balbina's skull was removed from her body and placed inside an ornate reliquary. This reliquary now resides in the Metropolitan Museum of Art in New York City.

4. The intercession of Potamiaena on behalf of Basilides constitutes one of the very first documented instances concerning the intercession of saints into the welfare of human souls.

5. Origen of Alexandria (184–253 AD), also known as Origen Adamantius, was an early Christian scholar, ascetic, and theologian who was born and spent the first half of his career in Alexandria. He was a prolific writer who wrote roughly 2,000 treatises in multiple branches of theology.. He was one of the most influential figures in early Christian theology and apologetics.

He was tortured for his faith during the Decian persecution in 250 AD and died three years later from his injuries. Roman emperor Justinian I condemned him as a heretic and ordered all his writings to be burned. The Second Council of Constantinople in 553 AD condemned certain heretical teachings which claimed to be derived from Origen. His teachings on the pre-existence of souls were rejected by the Church.

6. For that, she was later declared to be the patron saint of music and musicians.

7. Cecilia is one of the most famous of the Roman martyrs, and one of several virgin martyrs commemorated by name in the Canon of the Mass in the Latin Church.

8. The crypt of Saint Agatha is now an underground basilica, which from early ages was venerated by the people of Malta. At the time of Agatha's stay, the crypt was a small natural cave, but during the 4th and 5th century, it was enlarged and embellished.

9. Tallow is the thick fatty oil of oxen and sheep.

10. the gate and the road leading from Rome to Ostia.

11. where there now stands the 'Church of Saint Prisca'

12. Saint Barbara is often portrayed with miniature chains and a tower. As one of the 'Fourteen Holy Helpers', Barbara continues to be a popular saint in modern times because of her association with lightning, which killed her father. She is sometimes credited with 13 miracles.

13. Reference Daniel chapter 3.

14. the first Coptic Orthodox monastery for men and women

15. During the reign of emperor Constantine the Great, his mother Helena visited the site of Demiana's monastery, and had a church built over the tomb. The original monastery and church were eventually destroyed by fire and storm, but a new complex was built and still stands on the very same site to this day. Saint Demiana's Monastery was officially consecrated as a Coptic Orthodox Monastery for nuns in 1978. Presently on the complex property, four of the nine churches bear her name: Saint Demiana's Big Church, Saint Demiana's Tomb Church, Saint Demiana's Ancient Church, and Saint Demiana's Church for Nuns. Every year, many people visit Saint Demiana's shrine, asking for her intercessions. Saint Demiana is the founder of monasticism for Coptic Orthodox nuns and the highest-ranking female martyr of the Coptic Orthodox Church, due to her forbearance of great persecution, torture, and suffering. Many churches in the greater Coptic Orthodox Church bear her name.

In May 2014, Egyptian security forces narrowly averted a car bomb attack on the monastery.

16. Of course, most emperors and high officials played this game with many such young women. However, once the novelty was worn off and the woman became an annoyance, she would be quickly discarded for a newer model. The time period could be as short as a few months depending upon the ruler's ego, sexual appetite, and thirst for power.

17. A miracle accepted as proved in 1833 was the multiplication of the bone dust of the saint, which provided for hundreds of reliquaries without the original amount supposedly experiencing any decrease in quantity.

18. This is the reason why Lucy is the patron saint of those with eye illnesses.

19. Lucy's memorial feast day falls at the darkest time of the year, the 13th of December.

20. The town is sometimes referred to as Abitina or Albitina.

21. Restituta is the patron saint of Lacco Ameno, and is especially venerated on the is island of Ischia, where she is celebrated in a 3-day celebration every year. 'Saint Restituta Church' was built in her honor in Naples in the 6th century, and was incorporated into the Cathedral of Naples built on the same site in the 13th century. A crypt associated with Restituta can be found at Cagliari, in the neighborhood of Stampace.

22. Saint Margaret is one of the '14 Holy Helpers'.

23. It should be noted that there is no direct evidence that Catherine herself was a historical figure – she may well have been a composite drawn from memories of women persecuted for their faith. However, she is considered a highly regarded saint, and the most important of the virgin martyrs (a group including Agnes of Rome, Margaret of Antioch, and Lucy of Syracuse), becoming the patroness of young maidens and female students. Looked upon as the holiest and most illustrious of the virgins of Christ after the Blessed Virgin Mary, it was natural that she, out of all the others, would be worthy to watch over the virgins of the cloisters and the young women of the world. Her power as an intercessor was renowned in the late Middle Ages.

24. Catherine is traditionally revered as one of the '14 Holy Helpers'.

25. Some modern scholars think that the legend of Catherine was based on the life and murder of the Greek philosopher Hypatia of Alexandria (who died in 415 AD), with reversed roles of Christians and pagans. Hypatia was a Greek mathematician, astronomer, and philosopher, who was murdered by a Christian mob after being accused of exacerbating a conflict between two prominent figures in the city, the governor Orestes, and the bishop Cyril. The idea that Catherine's life was either based on, or became confused with, the life of the pagan Hypatia has become a controversial theory among modern scholars.

26. See Endnote 6 above.

27. The quick and relatively painless execution method of beheading was usually reserved for the last, if other methods did not result in death. All other more spectacular methods (beasts, burning, bone-breaking, lacerating, etc.) were preferred at first, to rile up the spectators and to increase the suffering of the victim.

28. In the 6th century, the eastern Roman emperor Justinian established what is now Saint Catherine's Monastery at the foot of Mount Sinai in Egypt (which is in fact dedicated to the Transfiguration of Christ). Alleged rediscovery of her body here occurred about 800 AD, supposedly with hair still growing and a constant stream of healing oil issuing forth. Countless people make the pilgrimage to the Monastery every year to receive miracle healing from Catherine. Pilgrims are given a ring that has been placed on the relics of the saint as a blessing in remembrance of their visit. Many other scattered shrines and altars dedicated to Saint Catherine in France and England claim to have some of her relics.

29. The Council of Chalcedon, the Fourth Ecumenical Council of the Christian Church, took place in the city of Chalcedon in the year 451 AD. It repudiated the doctrine of monophysitism (which asserted that Jesus had only one nature [that being divine] and not two natures), and set forth the orthodox doctrine (the 'Chalcedonian Definition'), which described the 'full humanity and full divinity' of Jesus Christ, the Second Person of the Holy Trinity. Present at the council were 630 representatives from all the local Christian churches. The meetings were quite contentious, and no decisive consensus could be reached. At the end, both parties wrote a scroll of confession of their faith and placed it on the breast of Saint Euphemia within her tomb. After three days the tomb was opened and the scroll with the orthodox confession was seen in the right hand of Saint Euphemia while the scroll of the monophysites lay at her feet.

30. Ares was the Greek god of War, also known as Mars in the Roman pantheon.

31. The 'breaking wheel' or 'execution wheel', also known as the 'Catherine wheel' (because of its association with Saint Catherine of Alexandria), or simply as 'the wheel', was a torture device used for public execution from antiquity. It was a method used to break the bones of the accused and crush them to death, often causing prolonged torture spanning multiple days. Victims who faced torture and death through this device were said to be 'broken on the wheel'. It consisted of a large wooden wagon wheel which consisted of several radial spokes. A condemned person was lashed to the wheel and a club or iron cudgel was used to beat their limbs and break the bones. The victim's body, after his death, could also be displayed on the wheel. The present-day sputtering Catherine-wheel firework is loosely modeled after this torture device.

32. Bithynia was a Roman province in northern Turkey along the Black Sea coast from Istanbul on eastward. The apostle Paul was planning to continue his missionary work here, but was instead directed into Europe by the Holy Spirit (or the spirit of Jesus). Acts 16:6-10.

33. Some of the relics of the holy martyrs are preserved on Mount Athos, Greece, in the Protection cathedral of the Saint Panteleimon Russian monastery. The hand of Saint Metrodora is in the monastery of the Pantocrator.

34. For more on bishop Anthimus (or Anthony), see the section 'Early Fourth Century Persecution' in chapter 2 of this book.

35. The '10,000 Martyrs of Nicomedia' may be an embellished term. However, estimates ranged up to 20,000 in the 5th to 7th century. Most scholars today believe the number is probably less than 10,000. See Endnote 42 in chapter 2 of this book.

7 THE HEROIC SLAVE WOMEN

Saint, Martyr, Slave

Married or unmarried, the female slave deserves a special place in martyrdom history. Rising from the very bottom to the very top required a massively strong inner strength and conviction. Faith, freedom, and virtue, equally threatened, were overcome by saintly passion and surrender. To recognize them is to admire them. But to remember them is to honor them.

THE FORGOTTEN HEROES

Seraphia of Rome (~119 AD)
(see chapter 3)
Zoe of Pamphylia (~127 AD)
(see chapter 3)

Ariadne of Phrygia (~130 AD)

Ariadne was a slave in the household of a prince of Phrygia, a Roman province in central Anatolia (modern-day Turkey). Because of her Christian faith, she refused to participate in sacrificial rites to a pagan god, as part of the prince's birthday celebration. Because of this, she was beaten and handed over to Roman officials on charges of disobedience to her owner and disrespect to the gods. But she managed to free herself from the officials holding her and ran away from the household into the countryside. Of course, she was pursued by the authorities, and eventually found in a hilly glen not too far away. Just as she was about to be apprehended, she fell into a tiny hollow in the ravine and was never seen again – the assumption being that she was entombed in the rock.[1]

Agathoclia of Aragon (~230 AD)

(see chapter 3)

Sabina the Slave (~250 AD)

In an act of punishment and intimidation for failing to properly revere the Roman gods as commanded, a Christian slave named Sabina was bound and abandoned in the nearby mountains by her pagan mistress, who was attempting to 'teach her a lesson'. The owner wanted to change the girl's way of thinking (her faith) and force her to be more obedient. The plan was to let her suffer for a few days and then bring her back, humbled and changed from her old ways.

But Sabina freed herself and hid to prevent recapture. Searchers were sent to find her, but she didn't want to go back – she didn't want further punishment, but she didn't want to change her religious convictions either. She kept running and hiding, just out of reach of the pursuers. She was fortunate to find a friendly underground Christian community who secretly gave her food and money. They even contacted the pagan owner and made heroic efforts to legally free her from her bondage and servitude. But the mistress was resolute and hired bounty hunters to find not only her servant, but also the underground Christians. The search was relentless, and eventually Sabina was found and the Christians scattered.

The owner then had Sabina brought before the official prosecutors, with hopes that she would repent. But Sabina would not give in to her evil mistress or to the cruel threats from the judge. In the end, she was found guilty and convicted. Torture followed as expected and Sabina expired quickly. She willingly chose death as a martyr rather than subjugation to the pagan mistress with her pagan gods. Instead, she chose the glorious life in heaven in service to Jesus Christ.[2]

Basilissa and Kalliniki (~252 AD)

A wealthy Christian widow in the Roman province of Galatia,[3] Basilissa wanted to give money to the Christians who were incarcerated in prison there for their faith. Although not allowed to give food or clothing, it was possible to slip them some money during visiting hours when no one was looking. This would give them encouragement and hope for the future. In turn, they could slip it to their families or to the church, along with their prayers. Basilissa knew that many of these prisoners were destined for martyrdom, and they needed understanding and reassurance. Clipped to the currency bills was a note that said, "Stay the course – your reward will be in heaven."[4]

Basilissa would give the money (along with instructions) to her young servant girl Kalliniki,[5] who would go to the prison and secretly distribute it to the Christians who were confined there.

One day, Kalliniki was discovered and arrested. They asked her why she was giving money to the prisoners, since it was illegal. She said that it was for their future in heaven. This didn't make any sense to the authorities, so they asked her who had told her to do this. Unable to lie, Kalliniki told them that her mistress had given her the money. Then, she was tied up and thrown in a jail cell. Naturally, they found Basilissa a short time later and she also was arrested.

The next day, the two women were brought before the judge in court and charged with abetting the prisoners. But both women boldly confessed that they were Christians, and had a duty to help fellow Christians in need. Very quickly, they were found guilty of not worshipping the gods, and were sentenced to various tortures, in an attempt to make them deny their faith.

However, under the protection of God, the tortures were ineffective and neither Basilissa or Kalliniki could be persuaded to renounce their faith or to offer a penitent sacrifice to the pagan idols. Consequently, they were both beheaded by the sword that very day. May their souls rest in peace in the Kingdom of Heaven.

Flora and Lucilla of Rome (~260 AD)

Sisters Flora (also known as Fiora) and Lucilla were two of 23 Christians martyred together in Rome in the persecutions of emperor Gallienus. They had been kidnapped and enslaved by Saint Eugene of Rome before his conversion to Christianity, but were freed after his conversion.

Julia of Troyes (~273 AD)

Julia was captured as a spoil of war by the forces of Roman emperor Aurelian following their victory over Tetricus. She was given as a prize to Claudius of Troyes, France, an army officer. However, she converted him, and they were martyred together by beheading.

Mary the Slave (~300 AD)

Mary was a hard-working Christian slave in the house of Tertullus, a pagan patrician in Rome. She was accused and delivered to the local governor on charges of being a Christian during the persecutions of emperor Diocletian. Despite Tertullus' valiant efforts to save her, Mary suffered so many horrible tortures that local citizens demanded that she be released. The governor then turned over the custody of her to a soldier who he thought needed a slave, even though she was considered 'damaged goods'. However, the soldier helped her to escape from the city and disappear into the mountains. Legend has it that she lived a long life and died a natural death. However, she is venerated as a martyr because of the intensity of her sufferings and intention to sacrifice her life.

Laurentia of Ancona (~302 AD)

Laurentia was the wet nurse or slave, of an aristocratic Roman woman living in Ancona, Italy, named Palatias (Palatia). Laurentia converted her mistress Palatias, to Christianity, and they were both martyred in Fermo, Italy, during the persecutions of emperor Diocletian. The story of their lives and martyrdom contain many of the same legendary tales as found in the accounts of other virgin saints, such as Saint Christina and Saint Barbara. A church and a monastery were built in their honor in Ancona.[6]

Engratia, Julia, and the Martyrs of Zaragoza (~303 AD)

Engratia was a native of Braga, Spain, who had been promised in marriage to a nobleman of Roussillon in Gaul. Escorting her from Braga to Gaul was her uncle Lupercius,[7] a suite of 16 noblemen, and a servant girl named Julia (or Julie).

Upon reaching Zaragoza (Saragossa), they learned of the persecution of Christians there by a man named Dacian, who was the governor of the region during the reign of co-emperors Diocletian and Maximian. Engratia obtained a hearing before the governor, where she attempted to dissuade him from his persecution. But Dacian was not willing to listen, and instead had her whipped and imprisoned. When it was discovered that she was a Christian, she was tortured severely. She died of her wounds in prison. Julia and the other travelling companions were all beheaded as Christian accomplices.

Many others, called the 'Martyrs of Zaragoza',[8] were martyred during this time of intense persecution.

Devota of Corsica and Monaco (~303 AD)

A young Corsican woman who had decided to devote herself fully to the service of God, Devota became a servant or slave in the household of the Roman senator Eutychius. When the governor Barbarus arrived in Corsica with a fleet of ships, he learned that the senator was harboring a Christian in his house. He demanded that she be given up and compelled to perform the requisite sacrifice, but Eutychius refused. Not wanting to confront him directly, Barbarus simply had him poisoned. Devota was then imprisoned and tortured for her faith – her mouth was crushed, and her body was dragged through rocks and brambles. She was eventually executed by being racked and stoned to death.

After her death, the governor ordered for her body to be burned to prevent its veneration. However, it was saved from the flames by local Christians, who placed the body on a boat bound for Africa, where it was believed it would receive proper Christian burial. However, a storm overtook the boat, and it was guided (some say by a dove) to the present-day port of Les Gaumates, in the Principality of Monaco.[9]

Leocadia of Toledo (~304 AD)

Leocadia was a young slave who was beaten and imprisoned for refusing to denounce her faith during the persecutions of emperor Diocletian. Scheduled for torture, and then either apostasy or martyrdom, she learned of the abuse being suffered by a 13-year-old girl in Merida, Spain, named Eulalia.[10] Leocadia could not bear living in a world where such evil occurred, and so she prayed to God to remove her from this world and all the evil in it. She died shortly thereafter, of unknown causes without having to face the torturers. She is considered a saint because of her strength of faith and prayer, and is thought to have been called to heaven supernaturally.

Charitina of Amisus (~304 AD)

(also known as Charitina of Rome)

Distinguished by her strict chastity and piety, Charitina spent her life in fasting, prayer and study. Orphaned young, she was the servant of an eminent Christian man called Claudius the pious, who brought her up as his own daughter. The young woman was very pretty, sensible, and kind. She imparted her love for Christ to others, and by her example she converted many to the true way of salvation. Charitina was meek, humble, obedient and silent. Although not as yet baptized, she was a Christian at heart, and studied the law of God day and night. She vowed to live in perpetual virginity as a true bride of Christ.

However, word got out that she had Christian leanings and was bringing others to the Christian faith. The regional governor, Dometius, heard about her and sent soldiers to forcibly seize her from her home and bring her to trial.

In the courtroom, the judge asked her: "Is it true, little

girl, that you are a Christian, and that you delude others by bringing them to this dishonorable religion?" To this, Charitina courageously replied:

It is true that I am a Christian, and a lie that I delude others. I lead those in error to the Way of Truth, bringing them to the Path of Christ.

The judge was not amused. He ordered that her hair be cut off and hot coals be dumped on her head, but the maiden was preserved by God's power. They threw her into the sea, but by God's will she swam to shore and stood up, exclaiming, "Now I have been baptized." She was bound to a torture wheel which began to turn, but by God's word the wheel jammed, and Charitina remained unharmed. Then the wicked judge sent some dissolute youths to rape her. Fearing this dishonor, Charitina prayed to God to receive her soul before these vile men could foul her virginal body. And thus it was: while she was kneeling in prayer, her soul went out from her body to the immortal Kingdom of Christ. The angry heathens desecrated her body and then threw it into the sea. But Charitina had died a martyr's death and was one with God in heaven.

Maxima of Rome (~304 AD)

Maxima was a nurse/slave in Rome who secretly baptized Saint Ansanus.[11] She was scourged, along with Ansanus, for stealing and secretly burying the body of Saint Lucy and for professing Christianity, during the persecutions of emperor Diocletian. Maxima died from the scourging, but Ansanus lived and went on to evangelize in Siena, Italy.

Ligna, Eunonia, and Eutropia (~304 AD)
(The Slaves of Saint Afra)

It is not expressly known whether these slaves had been converted to Christianity before execution, or whether they were just following direction from their owner. In truth, it may have been a little of each. They were probably present when Bishop Narcissus of Augsburg converted Afra and her mother Hilaria, and heard the sermonizing; or they may have been subsequently evangelized by Hilaria or Afra; or they may have just listened, nodded, and then ignored everything that had been said. Like most slaves, it would depend on the personal relationship they had with their master, along with their own inner convictions.

Dula the Slave (~307 AD) (also called Theodula)

The virgin martyr Dula was the Christian slave of a pagan soldier in Nicomedia, Asia Minor. She died by stabbing, fighting off a rape attempt by her evil owner.

NOTES

1. Legend has it that a crack in a large rock opened up just wide enough for her to squeeze into and get away. So, it wasn't a fall, it was an escape. But she was caught in the rock some distance away and couldn't get out.

2. "The Martyrdom of Pionius", in Herbert Musurillo, *The Acts of the Christian Martyrs* [Oxford: University Press, 1972]

3. A region in central Turkey, today

4. We don't know exactly what the note said. In effect, it was a plea not to lose their courage amid the coming tribulations - to not renounce the faith and lose their future life in heaven.

5. Whether Kalliniki was legally a servant or a slave is unknown, but a slave would be a good guess. Either way, Kalliniki appears to be very acquiescing to Basilissa. Putting a servant into such a dangerous situation poses many probing questions. The name Kalliniki is of Greek origin, meaning "beautiful victor", in feminine form.

6. Their relics of Laurentia and Palatias were collected in one small bronze urn, and donated to Ancona Cathedral by Pope Benedict XIV, who had been bishop of that city.

7. sometimes identified with Luperculus, who was a bishop of Eauze

8. Also called the 'Countless Martyrs of Zaragoza', there were actually two groups of martyrs. The first group consisted of 17 men and 2 women (with 2 survivors). The second group was too numerous to count.

9. The 'Legend of Saint Devota' is one of the Principality of Monaco's oldest traditions – it has influenced the national culture in fields as diverse as religion, customs, history, literature, the arts, painting, music, coins, and stamps. The legend holds a special place in the heart of Monaco's people, and over the centuries has been awarded a permanent place in the city's history.

Regrettably, many young people today only know of the name by its association with Monaco's Grand Prix Formula 1 race, and the famous 'bend of Saint Devota' that is endlessly quipped by radio and TV commentators.

10. Saint Eulalia is a venerated 12-13 year old virgin martyr from Merida, Spain (who may be the same person as Saint Eulalia of Barcelona).

11. Saint Ansanus the Baptizer, called 'The Apostle of Siena', died in 304 AD and is the patron saint of Siena, Italy.

8 THE LESSER HEROES

Less Sensational but Not Less Heroic

They are women and they were all martyrs (although in some cases, the martyrdom is uncertain). Many are classified as saints, but not all. Many were young, some were old. Some were unmarried, some were married. Some were rich and many were poor. But they all have a story – a story that deserves to be remembered. Unfortunately, history, record-keeping, and time have combined to blur the truth of the stories. The major Christian denominations keep a record, but the veracity of the record is problematic. Nevertheless, the truth of their stories is known to God in Heaven, and their place in the Kingdom is forever.

The following listing in chronological order (but remember, all dates are best estimates), is a brief summary of the less sensationalized heroes. It is not comprehensive or definitive. But it is a good reference for a quick look at names, dates, places, and events – as a starting place for further reading and research. Obviously, a 1- or 2-liner does not do justice to the suffering involved, but space and time are limited in this book. Nevertheless, they are real heroes, and they must not be forgotten.[1]

The common listed name, date, and place of martyrdom are given, along with an informational tidbit of the situation.

THE UNSUNG HEROES

Apphia of Colossae (68 AD) Turkey – wife of Philemon [2]–
martyred with Philemon, Archippus, and Onesimus [3]

Constanza (Constantia) of Campania (68 AD) Italy – martyr –
executed with brother

Zenaida and Philonella of Thessaly (100 AD) Greece – sisters –
cousins of St. Paul – physicians – martyrdom uncertain

Hermione of Ephesus (117 AD) Turkey – daughter of Philip [4]–
tortured with intent to execute, but lived to die at peace

Theodora of Rome (120 AD) – virgin martyr –
executed for giving aid to her brother in prison

Fides, Spes, Caritas (128 AD) Rome – Faith, Hope, and Charity –
virgin martyrs – mystical baptismal names; actual names unknown

Justa, Justina, and Henedina of Sardinia (130 AD) – virgin martyrs –
sisters executed for professing Christianity

Symphorosa of Tivoli (138 AD) Italy – martyred mother of 7 sons [5]–
thrown into the river with a heavy rock fastened to her neck –
all 7 sons martyred the next day [6]

Oliva (Olivia) of Brescia (138 AD) Italy

Mariña, Quiteria, Liberata, and Euphemia (139 AD) Portugal –
virgin martyrs and insurrectionists [7]– 4 of 'The Nonuplet Sisters'

Antia (140 AD) Rome – martyred with son –
beheaded as her son was clubbed to death

Venera (Veneranda) (143 AD) – virgin martyr –[8]
missionary in Sicily, Italy, Greece, and France, converting many –
arrested and tortured by 3 different governors – nailed on a cross,
boiled in oil, and eventually beheaded

Felicitas of Rome (164 AD) – martyred mother of 7 sons [9]–
mother and all sons martyred –

Praxedes and Pudentiana (165 AD) Rome – virgin martyrs –
sisters executed as Christian evangelists – Pudentiana age 16

Corona (Stephania) (170 AD) Syria – age 16 martyr –
wife of an unknown Roman soldier –
arrested and executed for comforting another soldier after torture

Albina (173 AD) Rome – virgin martyr –
executed with brother

Glyceria of Thrace (177 AD) Greece – virgin martyr –
died just prior to being torn apart by wild animals –
the 'Oil of Saints' oozed from her body

Paraskevi of Rome (180 AD) – virgin martyr –[10]

Donata, Secunda, Vestia, Januaria, Generosa (180 AD) Tunisia –
virgin martyrs as part of a group persecution –
5 of 'The Scillitan Martyrs' of Carthage

Martina of Rome (228 AD) – virgin martyr [11]–
noble and beautiful orphaned daughter of a Roman ex-official –
scourged, burned, and finally beheaded

Tatiana of Rome (231 AD) – virgin martyr [12]– deaconess –
beaten and beheaded

Apollonia (247 AD) Alexandria – virgin martyr –
mob persecution – all her teeth smashed, then burned to death

Quinta (247 AD) Alexandria – martyr –
mob persecution – killed with a companion

Cyriaca (Dominica) (249 AD) Rome – martyred widow –
scourged to death for befriending other Christians

Agathonica of Pergamum (250 AD) Turkey – martyr –
executed with her brother (a deacon) and the local bishop –
hanged and burned, defending the others [13]

Vibiana (250 AD) Rome – virgin martyr [14]

Vincenca (Vicenza) (250 AD) Rome – age 16 virgin martyr –
tortured and executed for expressing Christianity

Reparata (250 AD) Palestine – age 15 virgin martyr –[15]
burned, choked with boiling pitch, and finally beheaded for refusal to
sacrifice

Victoria and Anatolia (250 AD) Italy – virgin martyred sisters –
rejected arranged marriages – converted their jailor after saving him
from a poisonous snake – all 3 stabbed through the heart

Kalliopi (Calliope) (250 AD) Greece – virgin martyr –
tortured at request of spurned pagan suitors –
flogged, branded, and beheaded in the public square

Albina of Formia (250 AD) Italy – martyr [16]–
brought to Italy from Palestine

Anastasia the Roman (250 AD) – martyr –
a nun (heritage unknown)

Messalina of Foligno (250 AD) Italy – virgin martyr –
consecrated by the bishop – clubbed to death for providing care
during his imprisonment, and refusing to sacrifice to the pagan gods

Epicharis of Carthage (250 AD) Tunisia – martyred as a group –
executed with 11 other companions

Denise (Dionysia) (250 AD) Turkey – virgin martyr –
condemned a male apostate, who died shortly thereafter –
thwarted multiple rape attempts in prison –
beheaded after found burying the bodies of martyred friends

Regina (251 AD) France – age 15 virgin martyr –
tortured and beheaded for refusing to marry the local pagan proconsul

Euthalia (251 AD) Sicily – virgin martyr –
tortured and beheaded by her pagan brother for receiving Christian
baptism

Episteme (251 AD) Syria – martyr –
executed with husband (or fiancé) for refusing to sacrifice

Maxima, Donatilla, Secunda (257 AD) Tunisia – virgin martyrs –
ages 14, 16, and 12 respectively – beheaded after many tortures –
known as the 'Three Virgins of Tuburga'

Rufina and Secunda (257 AD) Rome – virgin martyrs –
daughters of a Roman senator – tortured and beheaded when fiancés
apostatized after persecutions started

Eugenia (258 AD) Rome – martyr – daughter of governor of Egypt –
baptized and became an abbot disguised as a man –
beheaded with her two chamberlains

Digna and Emerita (259 AD) Rome – martyrs

Agrippina of Mineo (262 AD) Sicily – virgin martyr –
blonde-haired beauty born of a noble Roman family –
scourged and beheaded in Rome; body moved to Sicily

Martha (270 AD) Rome – martyred with husband and 2 sons –
thrown into a well for burying the bodies of Christian martyrs –
husband and sons were beheaded

Restituta of Sora (271 AD) Italy – martyr

Columba of Sens (273 AD) France – virgin martyr –
saved from being burned at the stake by a female bear –
beheaded for refusing to marry the emperor's son

Mart Moura (283 AD) Egypt – martyred with husband, a deacon – crucified for refusing to convert to paganism when ordered to do so by the governor

Daria (283 AD) Rome – martyr [17]
originally a pagan 'vestal virgin' – was converted by her Christian husband, but remained chaste by agreement – sent to a brothel after husband was executed – buried alive in a deep pit [18]

Zoe of Rome (286 AD) – martyr –
a converted noblewoman, cured of dumbness by a Christian – hung over a fire, stifled by smoke, and thrown into the river

Alberta and Faith (Fe) of Agen (286 AD) France – martyrs –
earliest victims of Diocletian's persecution –
tortured and executed with a companion

Regula (286 AD) Zurich – martyr of the Theban Legion [19]–
beheaded with brother and servant after fleeing from the army regiment subject to execution for becoming Christians, and then being caught

Justa and Rufina of Seville (287 AD) Spain – martyred sisters –
pottery-makers age 17 and 19, who refused to sell their wares for use in a pagan celebration – smashed a statue of the goddess Venus [20]– endured multiple tortures, Justa dying from imprisonment without food or water; Rufina strangled, beheaded, and burned

Hripsime (Arsema) (290 AD) Armenia – virgin martyr, nun –
executed with teacher and 33 nuns of a virgin community [21]– tongue cut out, stomach cut open, and blinded before being roasted alive – body cut into pieces and fed to wild animals

Aquilina of Byblos (293 AD) Lebanon – 12 yr. old virgin martyr –
betrayed by a servant as a heathen teaching others – stripped, flogged, and metal rods drilled through her ears – beheaded as a sorceress after regaining consciousness and denouncing the governor

Susanna of Rome (295 AD) – virgin martyr –
  refused to marry a pagan relative of the emperor –
  beheaded in her father's house

Epicharis of Byzantium (300 AD) Turkey – martyr –
  wife of a Roman senator – scourged and then killed by the sword

Beatrix (Beatrice) (302 AD) Rome – martyr –
  betrayed by a neighbor 7 months after her 2 brothers were martyred –
  strangled in prison as the evil neighbor took possession of her land [22]

Palatias of Fermo (302 AD) Italy – martyr
  an aristocrat converted by her slave –
  both were executed for professing Christianity

Mohrael (Rais) [23] (303 AD) Egypt – 12 yr. old virgin martyr; healer –
  kidnapped and taken on a boat of Christian prisoners – beheaded after
  3 days torture with metal, fire, spiders, and venomous snakes [24]

Sophia, Pistis, Elpis, Agape (303 AD) Rome – Wisdom, Faith, Hope,
and Charity – mother and 3 virgin daughters all martyred –
  mystical baptismal names; actual names unknown

Justina of Antioch (303 AD) Turkey – virgin martyr –
  converted a pagan magician who dealt in sorcery – became the abbess
  of a convent, while the ex-magician became a bishop – both were
  tortured and beheaded for professing Christianity [25]

Marciana of Mauretania (303 AD) Algeria – virgin martyr –
  accused of having smashed a statue of the pagan goddess Diana –
  thrown to wild beasts in the amphitheatre – mauled by a leopard and
  gored to death by a bull

Paraskevi of Iconium (304 AD) Turkey – virgin martyr – [26]
  born to a rich Christian family, she became a preacher and converted
  many – accused and executed during the persecutions of Diocletian

Nympha (Ninfa) (304 AD) Sicily – virgin martyr –
fled from Palermo to the Italian mainland when the Goths invaded
Sicily – executed with 2 companions for professing Christianity [27]

Trofimena (Febronia) (304 AD) Sicily – 12 yr. old virgin martyr –
murdered by her father because she wanted to be baptized and become
a Christian [28]

Pelagia of Tarsus (304 AD) Turkey – virgin martyr –[29]
burned to death within a bronze bull, and her flesh melted,[30] for
refusing to marry the emperor's pagan son, and then the local pagan
governor

Honorina (304 AD) France – virgin martyr –
executed for professing Christianity during the persecutions – body
thrown into the Seine and drifted until reaching the banks,[31] where it
was collected by local Christians and buried in a tomb.

Justina of Padua (304 AD) Italy – virgin martyr –
mayor's daughter, devoted to Christianity – arrested and executed by
the sword for visiting prisons to comfort incarcerated Christians

Sarah of Antioch (304 AD) Syria – martyred with 2 sons –
burned to death with sons for refusing to reveal to her husband (and
to the authorities) how the boys had been baptized [32]

Emerentiana (304 AD) Rome – daughter of Agnes' wet nurse –
stoned to death for praying by Agnes of Rome's grave site, and
reprimanding the officials who asked her to leave

Anysia of Salonika (304 AD) Greece – virgin martyr –
apprehended on her way to mass by a Roman soldier, beaten, and
dragged to a pagan temple – murdered by the soldier for spitting in his
face when he tore off her veil (symbol of chastity vow)

Julitta (Julietta) of Tarsus (304 AD) Turkey – martyred with child –
beheaded after sides ripped apart with hooks – child thrown down
stairs and then beheaded [33]

Lucy of Rome (304 AD) – age 75 martyred widow –
accused by her son of being a Christian – placed in a cauldron of burning pitch, but survived – eventually beheaded along with a young catechist named Geminian, who she was teaching

Victoria, Thelica, Mary (Maria) of Carthage (304 AD) Tunisia –
3 of the 49 'Martyrs of Abitinae', that included ~20 women and 4 children (1 infant son) – Mary was a virgin martyr

Sotere (304 AD) Rome – virgin martyr –[34]
tortured and beheaded for disobeying orders to revere the Roman gods and to burn all other religious documents

Theodora (Antonina) of Alexandria (304 AD) [35]– virgin martyr –
forced to a brothel for refusing to wed a pagan, but rescued by a Christian man who traded clothes with her – both discovered shortly thereafter and executed by being burned alive

Anastasia of Sirmium (304 AD) Serbia [36]– virgin martyr –
healer and exorcist – beheaded for practicing Christian rituals, thought to be sorcery – known as the 'Deliverer from Potions'

Marcionilla (304 AD) Egypt – martyred mother of young son –
executed along with her son, a monk, a priest, and a catechist

Juliana & Barbara of Nicomedia (304 AD) Turkey – virgin martyrs–
refused marriage to a pagan – flogged, face burned with a hot iron, and finally beheaded [37]

Greca (304 AD) Sardinia – virgin martyr; nun –
imprisoned, whipped, and tortured (by having three nails hammered into her head) for professing Christianity

Eulalia of Merida (304 AD) Spain – age 12 virgin martyr –
stripped, flagellated, burned with torches, and crucified on an x-shaped cross for publicly denouncing the governor on his merciless persecution of Christians.[38]

Cantianilla (304 AD) Italy – orphan and martyr –
beheaded along with her 2 brothers for refusing to give sacrifice to
the pagan gods

Basilissa of Rome (304 AD) – virgin martyr; orphan –
refused arranged marriage claiming that she dedicated herself to God–
beheaded for refusing to marry and renounce her beliefs

Natalia of Nicomedia (306 AD) Turkey –
died in grief shortly after martyrdom of her just converted husband, a
top military official [39]

Antonia of Nicaea (306 AD) Turkey – martyr
insulted the pagan gods and refused to offer incense –stripped, hung
up by the arms, and sides of body torn with rakes –finally, placed in a
sack and drowned in a lake.

Theodosia of Tyre (307 AD) Palestine – age 17 virgin martyr –
deliberately sought inclusion with Christian martyrs –[40]
breasts and ribs torn with rakes until internal organs exposed –
finally, thrown into the sea

Domnina (310 AD) Syria – mother of 2 virgin daughters –
fearing rape and torture by soldiers after arrest for being Christian, all
3 jumped into the river and drowned themselves [41]

Munditia (310 AD) Rome – martyrdom uncertain –[42]
known as 'Munditia Protogenia', the Commendable – age 60

Dorothea (Dorothy) of Caesarea (311 AD) Palestine [43]– virgin martyr–
tried, tortured, and executed for professing Christianity

Fausta of Cyzicus (311 AD) Turkey – age 13 virgin martyr –
after many tortures, thrown into a cauldron of boiling water along with
her ex-executioner, who had converted after watching her courageous
resistance and accepting the faith [44]

Savina of Milan (311 AD) Italy – martyr –
killed for giving aid to Christian prisoners and ensuring that they
received proper burials after execution – died while praying at a
Christian tomb

NOTES

---

1. The listing is of female martyrs from 34 to 313 AD, underlined the individuals presented as 'Exalted Heroes' in chapter 5, 'Heroic Unmarried Women' in chapter 6, and 'Heroic Slave Women' in chapter 7. A full listing of all the heroes mentioned in this book (but not definitively complete) can be found in Appendix I.

2. see Philemon 2

3. Onesimus was the runaway slave who joined up with, and was converted by Paul, precipitating Paul's letter to Philemon (The Epistle of Paul to Philemon), asking that he be unpunished upon return. He did return, and stayed with Apphia and Philemon until the end, helping to preach the Gospel.

4. Hermione was one of four unmarried daughters of Philip the Evangelist (one of the Seven Assistants chosen in Jerusalem – see Endnote #11 in chapter 1), who were gifted with prophecy – see Acts 21:8-9. She and her sister Eutychia went to Ephesus in search of the Apostle John, but John had already died when they arrived. So, she became a disciple of Petronius, who was a disciple of Saint Paul. Philip and his two daughters were buried in the ancient city of Hierapolis (5 miles north of Laodicea and now just a ruin).

5. probably the same person as Felicitas of Rome

6. Being unsuccessful in his attempt to make the 7 sons sacrifice to the gods, the emperor ordered them to be tied to 7 stakes around the temple of Hercules. Their members were disjointed with a windlass (a winch used to lower buckets into, and hoist them up from, wells). Then, each was executed differently. Crescens was pierced through the throat, Julian through the breast, Nemesius through the heart, Primitivus was speared at the navel, Justinus was pierced through the back, Stracteus was pierced through the side, and Eugenius was cleft in two parts from top to bottom. Their bodies were thrown en-masse into a deep ditch employed for suicide victims and Christians suffering martyrdom.

7. Quiteria was the leader of the 'nonuplet sisters', who were named Eumelia (Euphemia), Liberata (Virgeforte), Gema (Mariña of Aguas Santas), Genebra, Germana, Basilissa, Marica, and Vitoria. They were born to an important Roman military official. Their mother, disgusted at the fact that she had given birth to nine daughters all at once (as if she were a common peasant, or an animal), ordered a maid to take them to a river to drown them. The father was unaware of their birth. The maid, however, gave the girls over to some local women who raised them up as Christians.

As adult women, they opposed the worship of Roman gods and were therefore brought before their father, who recognized them as his daughters. He wanted them to marry Roman officers, but they all refused – and were therefore imprisoned in a tower. Somehow, they managed to escape and liberate all the other prisoners in the tower. Then, they waged a guerrilla war in the mountains against the empire. Eventually, Quiteria, Euphemia, Liberata, and Mariña were apprehended and executed. The fate of the others is unknown.

8. probably the same person as Paraskevi of Rome

9. probably the same person as Symphorosa of Tivoli

10. probably the same person as Venera/Veneranda

11. probably the same person as Tatiana of Rome

12. probably the same person as Martina of Rome

13. Agathonica was a key witness in Carpus's trial. During the trial, she stripped herself naked in protest, claiming that she was just as guilty. After Carpus was put to death, she refused to sacrifice to the gods, even though the onlookers tried to persuade her, for the sake of her children. She shouted to them that "God will watch my children." She was then put to death by being hanged and burned.

14. Vibiana is the patron saint of the Archdiocese of Los Angeles, where some of her relics are housed. She is not to be confused with Bibiana (or Vibiana) of Rome, who was martyred in 363 AD.

15. Reparata is the patron saint of Nice and co-patron of Florence. Legend has it that her body was laid in a boat and blown by the breath of angels to a bay near Nice. Similar tales exist for Saint Restituta and Saint Devota.

16. possibly virgin martyr

17. Legend has it that that on the anniversary of their deaths, a large number of Christians gathered at their underground crypt to pay their respects. When a number of Roman soldiers surprised them, they were beaten, thrown into the crypt with stones, and buried alive, including a priest and a deacon.

18. Being buried alive was the chosen torment reserved for unfaithful vestal virgins.

19. For more on the Theban Legion, refer to the section on 'Third Century Persecution' in chapter 2.

20. after all their pottery was smashed by irate local residents

21. The sole survivor of the community massacre was a young girl named Nune (or Marine), who was later a missionary in Georgia and, as Saint Nino (Saint Christiana in western martyrologies), is praised as the founder of the Georgian Orthodox Church.

22. Divine punishment soon overtook the accuser and betrayer, who at a feast was mocking the folly of the martyrs. A small child cried out, "You have committed murder and have taken unjust possession of someone else's land! You are a slave of the devil!". Thereupon, the evil doer's soul was overtaken by Satan, and he was tortured for 3 hours before being cast into hell.

23. The two distinct individuals named in the records, Mohrael of Cairo and Rais of Antinoopolis, are probably the same person.

24. Legend has it that when the boat captain yelled, "I spit upon the Christian God," Mohrael/Rais objected, stepped up, and spat in the tyrant's face. Needless to say, she was put to death within the hour.

25. After the bodies of Justina and Cyprian (the 'magician') had lain unburied for 6 days, they were taken by Christian sailors to Rome, where they were interred on the estate of a noble lady named Rufina, and later were entombed in Constantine's basilica.

26. In Russia, Paraskevi (aka Paraskeva; Pyatnitsa) developed a unique and national personality. Icons depict her as an ascetic figure wearing the red of martyrdom, holding an Eastern cross, a scroll professing her faith, or a vessel that holds the perfume of martyrdom. She is the patron saint of traders and fairs, and of marriage.

27. Nympha may have actually died in the 6th century. Her relics have been preserved with the martyrs Tryphon and his companion Respicius, but she may not have been a co-martyr.

28. After death, Trofimena's body was hidden protectively in an urn and thrown into the sea, the current taking it to the coast of Italy and the town of Minori, where it was discovered by the locals. The subsequent history of Minori is tied directly to the cult and veneration of Trofimena, and for more than 1,000 years the town has jealously conserved her relics. An ancient church of Trofimena still exists in nearby Salerno, where all the remains were once housed, and where the top of her skull is still preserved.

Legend has it that when Minori was being attacked from the sea by Arab pirates, villagers invoked the intercession of Trofimena, and by a miracle, a terrible tempest rose up on an otherwise lovely summer day, and shipwrecked the attacking horde.

29. Pelagia of Tarsus may be confounded with Pelagia the Virgin, who was martyred around the same time, but was from Antioch. There is also some confusion with Pelagia the Harlot (aka Margarita; Pelagia of Antioch; Pelagia the Penitent), who was a repentant prostitute and hermit in the late 4th or 5th century.

30. Legend has it that the pagans sent four lions to devour her bones, but instead they protected the bones from vultures and crows, until a Christian bishop could recover them and give them a proper burial.

31. The body of Honorina drifted until reaching the banks of the river Seine, at a place now called Graville-Sainte-Honorine. Her relics were later moved to a chapel inside a castle, and when the castle was destroyed by barbarians, to a church outside the town walls of Conflans-Sainte-Honorine.

32. Unable to baptize her two sons in Antioch because of Christian persecutions, Sarah took them by boat to Egypt. On route, a great storm blew up, and fearful of her sons drowning unbaptized, she performed their baptisms herself – cutting her breast, marking the cross on their foreheads and over their hearts in her blood, and dipping them three times into the sea (in the name of the Father, Son, and Holy Spirit). Shortly thereafter, the storm died down, and the ship reached Alexandria. Sarah immediately took her sons to the bishop for official baptism, but when he went to perform the baptism , the water froze. After baptizing other children, he came back to Sarah's children to try again. But three times he tried, and three times the water froze. Whereupon, he exclaimed the profound saying:

It is indeed one baptism!

33. Other versions of the story say the child was age 3, or that the child was her son. Supposedly, the child stood up for the Christians and affronted the governor.

34. Sotere was supposedly a relative of Saint Ambrose. Her body was initially buried on the Appian Way, but was later transferred to the church of 'Saint Martin in the Mountains' in Rome.

35. The story of Saints Antonina and Alexander is nearly identical to that of Saints Theodora and Didymus. It's highly likely that Antonina and Theodora are the same person, and that Alexander and Didymus are the same person. Or it could be that one set of names is just a generic construct by a writer who didn't know the actual names. Or 'Antonina' and 'Alexander' may just be mnemonic device names that made oral repetition of the tale easier.

36. may have been a student of Saint Chrysogonus

37. The face-burning torture was done to Juliana. Afterwards, the torturer Eleusius sarcastically said, "Go now at the mirror to see your beauty". To this, Juliana replied:

At the resurrection of the righteous, there won't exist burnings or wounds, but only the soul. So, I prefer to have the wounds of the body which are temporary, rather than the wounds of the soul, which torture eternal.

Legend has it that Eleusius was later eaten by a lion, when he was shipwrecked on an unknown island.

The tortures imposed on Barbara are unknown.

38. Legend has it that Eulalia was placed in a barrel with shards of glass and rolled down a street, as part of her tortures. Note that Eulalia of Merida is probably the same person as Eulalia of Barcelona.

39. Adrian of Nicomedia (aka Hadrian) was a Herculean Guard of the Roman emperor and head of the praetorium. One day, while presiding over the torture of a group of Christians, he asked them what reward they expected to receive from their God. To which they replied:

Eye has not seen, nor ear heard, nor heart opened to, the things which God has prepared for them that love him.

He was so amazed at their courage that he publicly confessed his faith, though he had not yet been baptized. He was then immediately imprisoned and forbidden visitors. But his wife Natalia came to visit him, dressed as a boy, to ask the Lord for His grace when he entered Heaven. After his beheading, the executioner wanted to burn the body, but a storm arose and quenched the fire. Natalia recovered one of Adrian's hands and made a proper Christian burial.

Adrian was the chief military saint of Northern Europe for many years, second only to Saint George, and is much revered in Flanders, Germany, and northern France.

40. On Easter Day, Theodosia went to the public square where a number of Christians were in chains awaiting final sentencing. She honored them and asked to be remembered in their prayers. Seized by the guards and brought before the governor, she was ordered to sacrifice to the gods. When she refused, he had her tortured. But seeing that she endured the tortures uncomplainingly, he promised that if she sacrificed, then she would be released. But Theodosia was stoic. She replied that she had purposely gone to the square and spoken to the Christians under guard for the express purpose of being captured, and sharing in their martyrdom:

Why Sir, do you deceive yourself, and not perceive that at your hands, I have found the thing for which I have prayed to obtain? For I rejoice greatly in having been deemed worthy to be admitted to the holy place where God's martyrs endure sufferings for His Name. Indeed, for this very cause, I stood up and spoke with the Christians in chains, in order that by some means or other they might make me a partner in their sufferings.

Whereupon she was thrown into the sea.

Legend has it that the Christians she had spoken to, were sent away as slaves to work in the copper mines, without any tortures being inflicted on them. The governor had focused all of his fury on the young girl, and as a result, the others were neglected. In effect, Theodosia took the chains of the other Christian prisoners and hoisted them upon herself.

41. Other versions of the story say that Domnina alone jumped into the river, grabbing her daughters and pulling them in with her to prevent them from being raped.

42. The relics of Munditia reside in a side altar at Saint Peter's Church ('Old Saint Pete's') in Munich. They consist of a gilt-covered and gem-studded skeleton, located in a glass case, with false eyes in the skull (which is wrapped in netting). Jewels cover the mouth and rotted teeth.

43. Dorothy of Caesarea is known as one of 'The four Capital Virgins', the other three being Catherine of Alexandria, Margaret of Antioch, and the Great Martyr Barbara.

44. Legend has it that the magistrate, who condemned the first executioner, repented at the last moment and joined the pair in the cauldron.

COMMENTARY

IN general, Empires have better things to do than persecute monks, slaves, and nursing mothers. Powerful rulers tend not to care much about what people are doing as long as the servants are cleaning the house and cooking the food, taxes are collected, and no riots or unrest are occurring. But with regards to the cult of the Christians, something was anomalous – something weird about them. For a period of time, the persecution of Christians had been generally sporadic, local, improvised, and involved very few people. It was at the discretion of a regional governor to whom complaints were made by disgruntled citizens. It wasn't a dragnet or an imperial policy. Then, suddenly in the middle of the 3rd century, there was a policy shift. In the year 250 AD, the Emperor Decius decided that the Christian cult was a real threat to the Roman order, and that they had to be dealt with, empire-wide, with all the police power that the regime could muster. And so, he issued an official decree that everyone had to make a sacrifice to the Roman gods for the well-being of the empire. Furthermore, they also had to produce a certificate signed by a Roman official that verified that they had done so. Failure to do this, could have severe and brutal consequences.

In many places, Christianity, which had begun with tiny groups scattered in various cities across the empire, had now become a significant segment of the population. In some towns, they were even a majority. But they came palpably to the attention of the emperor because of their aloofness and counter-cultural tendencies. In the narrow view of the imperial office, these were the people who worshipped a man who had been crucified under Pontius Pilate, a Roman governor – and now they worshipped him as the son of a god, but not a Roman god. Obviously, they must be atheists, since they don't recognize the Roman gods. Furthermore, they seemed to engage in practices abhorrent to Roman customs, like incest, cannibalism, and orgies. Worst of all, they were becoming highly organized on an empire-wide basis, and not just on a local basis like other fringe religious communities. Clearly, they posed a threat to Roman stability. One can almost hear them murmuring behind closed doors something to the effect of: "This is dangerous – we can't have this large of a group doing things that could de-stabilize our society. Something has to be done about it...."

As a result of the spread of Christianity, a large number of Gentiles were now claiming the same religious exemption that the Jews had long had. Years ago, the Jewish authorities had come to a legal agreement with the Emperor that they would not be forced to participate in the pagan rituals that were part of the normal fabric of life in a Roman city. They were given a religious exemption as a gesture of imperial goodwill. But a Gentile who refused to participate had no legal standing. As a Gentile, the proper thing to do was to honor the gods of the empire. By not doing this, the Christians made themselves conspicuous, and invited the legal action of the Roman authorities. They became symbolic 'outlanders'. And therefore, they were used as a societal relief valve whenever political, social, or economic relief was needed in society.

The Hollywood view of Christianity as a persecuted underground society that skulked around in catacombs for three centuries before finally emerging 'out of the closet' after emperor Constantine's conversion, is not entirely true. Before the year 250 AD, persecution was sporadic, small scale, and often precipitated by local issues. However, the Christians were perceived as different. They turned away from the rituals and beliefs held by the general society, both religious and civic. They did not become involved in the more visible functions of society – they became aloof. This aroused suspicion among many of the prominent citizens. "Why don't the Christians participate in the rituals that are necessary to please the gods, and keep our society under their protection?" they wondered. There was suspicion that the Christians were trying to undermine the Roman society by their behavior. "If the Christians are not doing their duty to the gods, then why should the gods do anything good for the city?" they reasoned. And that was often the rationale for dragging Christians before the governor and accusing them of being troublemakers whenever there was a blip in the status-quo.

This was a time when the emperor was under great pressure. There was a lot of internal dissension, stacks of sheer corruption in the aristocracy (from the emperor on down), rampant inflation, and incredible governmental instability (driven by assassination or coup d'état, there were sometimes two or three emperors in a year.). There was also a sense that they were being besieged on the borders – that the barbarians were coming in at any moment. The Persians were dangerous, the Germans were dangerous, the Africans were dangerous, and so on – the empire was being battered on every frontier by invading armies. There was a pervasive feeling that anything that might upset the ancient contract between the Romans and the gods, was dangerous and had to be dealt with. The Christians were felt to be an internal threat to that contract. Something had to be done.

So, the Roman leaders bring to bear all the power they have at their disposal. They say, "OK, let's hit the leaders. Let's find these guys called bishops, bring them into court, and force them to recant by making a sacrifice to the emperor. If they refuse, we'll simply eliminate them and then follow the same process with all the followers." Consequently, many bishops and church leaders started fleeing to the countryside, while others were located, arrested, and tried. Ordinary people, for the first time, were rounded up, forced to sacrifice, and required to get a certificate of sacrifice (of course, the wealthier, or less steadfast, individuals could buy a forged certificate of sacrifice by bribing an official).[1] However, some believers absolutely refused to make the sacrifice, despite multiple attempts at trying to convince them to. Those who remained adamant, and loyal to the faith to the very end, were executed (following a pre-established protocol).

The policy was implemented with different degrees of rigor in different jurisdictions and by different local officials. Some were severe and some were lax. But it was a different veil of persecution that hung over the Christians than the sporadic oppression that was endured prior to the enactment of the imperial policy. There was a constant fear that 'you could be next'. The fear lingered and did not quickly abate. A second wave of official persecutions occurred under the emperor Diocletian around 303 AD.

Nevertheless, the Christians endured, and the net effect of it all is that a new cult of martyrs now appeared in Christianity. Feeding on existing anti-government sentiment, the Christian church actually became toughened and expanded. Many outsiders were brought into the Christian fold, and the morale of the people was strengthened – martyrs had become heroes and personifications of Christ, the first martyr. Consequently, the physical enforcements of the Decian and Diocletian persecutions did not last that long.

The martyrs were a heroic minority – they didn't represent a huge popular swelling. There were not tens of thousands of people being martyred. What we have, instead, is tens of thousands of people admiring the few who were martyred. In that sense, the martyr crossed 'the line in the sand', beyond which only the most saintly could cross. They achieved a spiritual height to be admired but not necessarily copied. Sometimes, there were pagans present at these martyrdoms who were so impressed by the bravery and courage of the Christians that they came to see the truth of the religion themselves, and converted to Christianity.

Overall, the stories of the martyrs had an incredible effect on the imagination of Christians – a regular person heroically witnessing to his own faith and against a hostile government – a hero emulating the life of Christ.[2] In general, the martyrdom accounts were written for other Christians to try to bolster their faith at a time of dreadful persecution – to keep up your courage in case it happened to you as well. However, the Christian leaders did not encourage people to volunteer themselves as martyrs.[3] Therefore, the general guidance from the church was that: 'It was OK not to volunteer yourself, but if you were apprehended, pressed, and really pushed to the wall, then you should not deny your faith'.[4]

There were many controversies surrounding what to do about people who denied, and then later wished to confess again. Some churchmen took a very lax line: "Well, people are repentant. We've all committed sins. They should just be forgiven and brought back in." Others took a kind of moderate line: "After a period of penance and public recantation and repentance, they should be allowed back into the church." And there were some hard-liners who thought that once you had renounced the faith by doing any one of those cowardly acts, there was no way for you to ever be a Christian again. Overall, there was a great deal of controversy among church people in this era, which went on for a long time.

After the enlightenment of emperor Constantine in 312 AD, there was an incredible blossoming of the cult of the martyrs. Shrines were built, liturgies were written, remains of the martyrs' bodies were distributed to churches, and there was an incredible desire to worship God near the relics of the martyrs. The era of the martyrs was closing (of course, sporadic martyrdom would continue for many more years),[5] but now the era of the heretics was just beginning.

Henceforth, most of the attacks on Christianity (with the exception of the Persian persecution – see Endnote 5) are intellectual in nature, as various ideological viewpoints and beliefs surface and resurface.[6] Different geographical regions were influenced to different extents by different heretical interpretations of the Gospel. Many of these challenges cut right to the core of the Christian faith, often resulting in bitter disputes (the ultimate definition of Christianity is itself challenged and debated over and over). But slowly over the years, the issues of contention are worked out (often not very amicably) and a canon of doctrine is slowly established. The Christian Church was beginning to become solidified and foundational. The 'rock' of Saint Peter had been firmly set in the ground.[7]

NOTES

1. There were various responses on the part of different Christian communities. You could have your slave or servant go to the stationhouse and do it for you (but he might also be a Christian, and who knows what he might do or not do), or you could pay your slave/servant and hope that he could buy two certificates, or you could pay the magistrate for the certificate but not actually do the sacrifice, if you could bribe him into not looking, or you could just go ahead and perform the sacrifice, rationalizing it by knowing that these gods are nothing but idols anyway. There were all sorts of different ways that people dealt with this. However, some people absolutely refused to obey the ruling at all. And those are the people, the heroic minority, who ended up being martyred by the imperial forces.

2. Polycarp was the bishop of Smyrna (which today is modern Izmir in Turkey), and at a very old age he was brought up for trial and persecution. He refused all attempts to get him to sacrifice, and he was martyred around 165 AD. In many aspects, his martyrdom mimicked the martyrdom of Jesus – there is a government official named Herod who's partly responsible – he is put upon a donkey and rides into the city – pagan officials try to get him to renounce his faith – to offer a pinch of incense to Caesar to show his reverence for the Roman emporium. But Polycarp refuses to do any of these things. And so, he is put to death by burning. After his death, his father collects his bones and saves them. This is one of the first instances that reveal the cult of the martyrs – the practice of preserving bits and pieces of the bodies of martyred people and holding them in great honor and esteem. Many of the martyrdoms after the time of Polycarp follow this same basic practice.

3. There are a few accounts in the historical records where in a fit of unbridled enthusiasm, a young Christian would run into the arena and yell, "Martyr me!" But when the angry wild beast came running toward him with glistening fangs, he quickly decided this wasn't such a good idea after all, and caved in to the oppressor's wishes. This brought a definite degree of shame and disgrace to Christianity.

4. After the two major persecutions of the third century and the early fourth century, there was a serious problem for the church because many Christians were not made of the same 'right stuff' (moral fiber) as the people who went to their death as martyrs. Perhaps under duress, they had disavowed the faith – by offering a sacrifice of incense to the emperor, or by bribing the officials to give them a certificate saying that they had offered the sacrifice, when in fact they had not. All of this posed a grave problem for the church when the persecutions were over because many of these people then wanted to come back into the church fold (this even included some bishops) – people were

asking pointed questions, like "were you truly baptized if you had been baptized by a bishop who fell away from the faith during the persecutions?"

5. Intense persecution continued especially in the regions east of the right bank of the Tigris River at the frontier between the Roman and the Persian Empires. The Persian persecution under King Shapur II was severe from 337-379 AD. The Christianization of the Roman Empire was especially distasteful and disruptive to the primarily Zoroastrian people of Sasanian Iran, since a great many Christians were living in the western regions of greater Persia, and their beliefs, practices, and behavior were upsetting the societal norms, just as had happened in the Roman Empire in the previous 300 years. Altogether, the common estimate of 16,000 martyrs is considered conservative by many – it may have been much greater.

6. There were many heresies faced by early Christianity. Principle among them were Gnosticism, Montanism, Arianism, Docetism, Nestorianism, Sabellianism, Manichaeism, Donatism, Ebionites, and Marcionism. For a more complete list of all the heresies, and how the church addressed them, refer to https://en.wikipedia.org/wiki/List_of_heresies_in_the_Catholic_Church.

7. Matthew 16:18

APPENDIX I

Index of Heroes

Chapter 2: First Century Persecution
Wife of the Apostle Peter
Eudokia of Heliopolis
Ephigenia of 'Ethiopia'

Chapter 3: Early Persecution of Women
Julia Livia
Thecla
Damaris
Pomponia Graecina
Claudia Rufina
Helena, daughter of Alphaeus
Basilissa and Anastasia
Petronilla and Felicula
Flavia Domatilla

Chapter 3: Martyrdom of Women Slaves
The Deaconesses of Bithynia
Zoe of Pamphylia
Felicitas of Carthage

Chapter 3: Martyrdom of Unmarried Women Slaves
Seraphia of Rome
Blandina of Lyons
Agathoclia of Aragon

Chapter 4: Freedom and Faith
Rufina and Secunda of Rome

Chapter 5: The Exalted Heroes
Blandina of Lyons
Perpetua and Felicitas of Carthage
Agape, Chionia, and Irene of Thessalonica

Chapter 6: The Heroic Unmarried Women
Balbina of Rome
Potamiaena of Alexandria
Cecilia of Rome
Agatha of Palermo
Prisca of Rome
Kyriaki of Nicomedia
Barbara of Nicomedia
Christina of Bolsena
Demiana of Egypt
Philomena of Rome
Lucy of Syracuse
Agnes of Rome
Victoria and Restituta of Africa
Margaret of Antioch
Catherine of Alexandria
Euphemia of Chalcedon
Menodora, Metrodora, and Nymphodora of Bithynia
Vasilissa of Nicomedia

Chapter 7: The Heroic Slave Women
Seraphia of Rome
Zoe of Pamphylia
Ariadne of Phrygia
Agathoclia of Aragon
Sabina the Slave
Kalliniki of Galatia
Flora and Lucilla of Rome
Julia of Troyes
Mary the Slave

Laurentia of Ancona
Julia of Zaragoza
Devota of Corsica
Leocadia of Toledo
Charitina of Amisus
Maxima of Rome
The Slaves of Afra
Dula the Slave

Chapter 8: The Lesser Heroes

Apphia of Colossae
Constanza (Constantia) of Campania
Zenaida and Philonella of Thessaly
Hermione of Ephesus
Theodora of Rome
Fides, Spes, and Caritas of Rome
Justa, Justina, and Henedina of Sardinia
Symphorosa of Tivoli
Oliva (Olivia) of Brescia
Mariña, Quiteria, Liberata, and Euphemia of Portugal
Antia of Rome
Venera (Veneranda) of Sicily
Felicitas of Rome
Praxedes and Pudentiana of Rome
Corona (Stephania) of Syria
Albina of Rome
Glyceria of Thrace
Paraskevi of Rome
Donata, Secunda, Vestia, Januaria, and Generosa of Tunisia
Martina of Rome
Tatiana of Rome
Apollonia of Alexandria
Quinta of Alexandria
Cyriaca (Dominica) of Rome
Agathonica of Pergamum

Vibiana of Rome
Vincenca (Vicenza) of Rome
Reparata of Palestine
Victoria and Anatolia of Italy
Kalliopi (Calliope) of Greece
Albina of Formia
Anastasia the Roman
Messalina of Foligno
Epicharis of Carthage
Denise (Dionysia) of Turkey
Regina of France
Euthalia of Sicily
Episteme of Syria
Maxima, Donatilla, and Secunda of Tunisia
Rufina and Secunda of Rome
Eugenia of Rome
Digna and Emerita of Rome
Agrippina of Mineo
Martha of Rome
Restituta of Sora
Columba of Sens
Mart Moura of Egypt
Daria of Rome
Zoe of Rome
Alberta and Faith of Agen
Regula of Zurich
Justa and Rufina of Seville
Hripsime (Arsema) of Armenia
Aquilina of Byblos
Susanna of Rome
Epicharis of Byzantium
Beatrix (Beatrice) of Rome
Palatias of Fermo
Mohrael (Rais) of Egypt
Sophia, Pistis, Elpis, and Agape of Rome

Justina of Antioch
Marciana of Mauretania
Paraskevi of Iconium
Nympha (Ninfa) of Sicily
Trofimena (Febronia) of Sicily
Pelagia of Tarsus
Honorina of France
Justina of Padua
Sarah of Antioch
Emerentiana of Rome
Anysia of Salonika
Julitta (Julietta) of Tarsus
Lucy of Rome
Victoria, Thelica, and Mary (Maria) of Carthage
Sotere of Rome
Theodora (Antonina) of Alexandria
Anastasia of Sirmium
Marcionilla of Egypt
Juliana and Barbara of Nicomedia
Greca of Sardinia
Eulalia of Merida
Cantianilla of Italy
Basilissa of Rome
Natalia of Nicomedia
Antonia of Nicaea
Theodosia of Tyre
Domnina of Syria
Munditia of Rome
Dorothea (Dorothy) of Caesarea
Fausta of Cyzicus
Savina of Milan

Honored Women of the Early Church Mentioned in Scripture

Acts 8:12 >>
Women are among the first Christian converts in Samaria, baptized by Phillip (probably before 40 AD).

Acts 11:13-15 >>
All the household of the Roman centurion Cornelius are saved by intervention of Peter.

Acts 16:9,11-15 >>
Paul has a vision of a man from Macedonia inviting him to come and help them. When he arrives in Philippi, he finds women gathered in a quiet place of prayer, and they listen to his preaching.

Acts 16:14-15 >>
The first baptized convert in Europe (at Philippi in Macedonia) is a woman named Lydia (originally from Thyatira in Asia Minor), a purveyor of purple cloth, who shows hospitality to Paul and Silas, and provides a meeting-place in her home for the infant church (51 AD). All of her household are baptized.

Acts 16:27-34 >>
All the household of the jailer in Philippi are baptized.

Acts 17:4 >>
Numerous prominent women in Thessalonica decide to become believers.

Acts 17:10-12 >>
Numerous influential Greek women in Beroea become believers.

Acts 17:34 >>
Damaris becomes a believer in Athens after listening to Paul's preaching.

Acts 18:8 >>
In Corinth, the whole household of Crispus become believers.

Acts 18:26 >>
Priscilla and her husband Aquila evangelize Apollos in Corinth.

Romans 16:1-2 >>
Paul commends Phoebe, deaconess of the church at Cenchrae, and asks that she be welcomed in Rome.

Romans 16:3-4 >>
Paul sends greetings to Priscilla and her husband Aquila, coworkers in service to Christ, and expresses his gratitude to them for risking their lives for the sake of his.

Romans 16:6,10-13,15 >>
Paul's closing salutation of this Epistle sends greetings to prominent women of faith who are active in the church at Rome:[1] Mary (who has worked hard), all those in the household of Aristobulus, all those in the household of Narcissus (who are in the Lord), Tryphena and Tryphosa (who worked hard for the Lord), Persis (who labored long in the Lord's service), the mother of Rufus (who was like a mother to Paul), Julia, and the sister of Nereus.

Romans 16:7 >>
Paul sends greetings to the woman Junia and the man Andronicus, kinsmen and fellow prisoners (outstanding apostles who became Christians even before Paul).

1 Corinthians 16:15 >>
Paul commends the household of Stephanas for being the first fruits of Achaia (mainland Greece) and devoted to the service of the saints.

Philippians 4:2-3 >>
Paul asks two women, Euodia and Syntyche, who actively struggled to promote the gospel with him, to come to a mutual understanding in the Lord – and he asks fellow believers to aid them in this.

2 Timothy 1:5 >>
Paul commends Lois and Eunice, grandmother and mother of Timothy, for their 'sincere faith', and for instructing Timothy in the Holy Scriptures.

2 Timothy 1:16 and 4:19 >>
Paul pleads for the Lord to have mercy on the family of Onesiphorus, and that they be greeted warmly by Timothy.

2 Timothy 4:19 >>
Paul asks Timothy to warmly greet Priscilla and Aquila.

2 Timothy 4:21 >>
Paul sends greetings to Timothy from Claudia, the mother of Linus, bishop of Rome. [2]

Philemon 2 >>
Paul sends greetings to Apphia, a sister in Christ Jesus at the church in Colossae.

2 John 1,4-5 >>
The writer (referred to as 'the elder') greets a lady who is elect, and her children – he commends the children walking in the path of truth, and requests that they love one another.[3]

2 John 13 >>
The writer sends closing greetings from the children of their elect sister.[4]

NOTES

1. The Christian faith community in Rome was probably originated by Jewish immigrants from Jerusalem who were Christian converts and left after the start of persecutions.

2. Many (but not all) historians believe that the Claudia mentioned here is Claudia Rufina, one of the 'saints of Caesar's household'. Wife of the Roman senator Aulus Pudens, and daughter of a British king, it is thought that she is the mother of Linus, Peter's successor as Bishop of Rome. See chapter 3.

3. The elder was using an accepted literary device – personifying a Christian community as a woman, and the church members as her children.

4. 'your elect sister' means the church community where the elder resides.

The Last Dreams of Perpetua

Perpetua's Dream, Part 1:

I saw a ladder of tremendous height made of bronze, reaching all the way up to the heavens – but it was so narrow that only one person could climb up at a time. To the sides of the ladder were attached all sorts of metal weapons – swords, spears, hooks, daggers, and spikes – so if anyone tried to climb up carelessly or without paying attention, he could easily be injured, and his flesh torn by the weapons. At the foot of the ladder lay a dragon of enormous size. It would attack those who tried to climb up, and try to terrify those who were unsure.

Saturus was the first to climb up – this gentle man who was later to give himself up of his own accord. He had been the builder of our strength, although he was not present when we were arrested. When he arrived at the top of the staircase, he looked down and called to me, "Perpetua, I am waiting for you. But take care – do not let the dragon bite you."

"He will not harm me," I said, "in the name of Christ Jesus."

Slowly, as though he were afraid of me, the dragon stuck his head out from underneath the ladder. Without hesitation, I jumped on his head, and using it as my first step, went on up.

At the top I saw an immense garden, and in it sat a gray-haired man wearing shepherd's clothes. He was tall and milking a sheep. Standing around him were many thousands of people clad in white garments. He raised his head, looked at me, and said, "I am glad you have come, my child."

He called me over to him and offered me some of the milk he was drawing. I took it in my cupped hands and consumed it gratefully. And all those who stood around said, "Amen!"

At the sound of this word, I awakened from the vision, with the taste of something sweet still in my mouth.

Perpetua's Dream, Part 2:

Pomponius, the deacon, came to the prison gates and began to knock loudly. I went out and opened the gate for him. He was dressed in an unbelted white tunic, wearing elaborate sandals.

He said to me, "Perpetua, come – we are waiting for you."

Then, he took my hand and we began to walk through the wild and rugged countryside. At last, we came to the amphitheatre out of breath, and he led me into the centre of the arena.

"Do not be afraid," he told me. "I am here, struggling with you." And then he left.

I looked around at the enormous crowd, who were watching me with astonishment. I was surprised that no beasts were let loose, for I thought that I was condemned to die by the beasts. Then, out came an Egyptian fellow of vicious appearance, together with his assistants, to fight against me. But some handsome young men also came out to stand with me, as my assistants.

Suddenly, my clothes were stripped off, and I noticed that I looked like a man. My assistants began to rub me down with oil (as they normally do before a contest). Looking over to the other side of the arena, I saw the Egyptian man rolling in the dust, preparing for battle.

Next, there appeared a giant of marvelous stature, rising above the top of the amphitheatre. He was clad in a beltless purple tunic with two stripes (one on either side) running down the middle of his chest. He wore sandals that were wondrously made of gold and silver. He carried a wand like an athletic trainer, and a green branch on which there were golden apples growing.

He commanded the crowd to be silent, and said, "If this Egyptian can defeat the woman, he will slay her with the sword. But if she defeats him, she will receive this branch of green and gold." Then he withdrew.

The Egyptian and I drew close to one another and began to let our fists fly. My opponent tried to get hold of my legs, but I kept striking him in the face with the heels of my feet. Then, he raised me up into the air, and I began to pummel him without my feet touching the ground. When I noticed there was a lull in his attack, I put my two hands together, linking the fingers of one hand with those of the other, and managed to get hold of his head. Pushing downwards, he fell flat on his face – and so I stepped on his head!

The crowd began to shout and my assistants started to sing psalms. So, I walked up to the giant and took the branch of green and gold. He kissed me and said, "Peace be with you, my daughter!" I began to walk in triumph towards the Gate of Life, but then suddenly I awoke.

It was then that I realized that the real fight in my life would be against the Devil, and not against the wild animals. I also knew that I would win the victory!

About the Author:

Edward N Brown is a storyteller with a background in science, philosophy, theology, and engineering. His technique is to blend the interesting nuggets of history, myth, science, biography, design, romance, poetry, spirituality, and personal drama – all mixed together into an informative, but easy-reading, faith-based tale of inspiration and wonder. Years of personal study exploring the great mysteries that connect the secular with the spiritual, coupled with an educational background of three advanced degrees (PhD + two MS) with a focus on systems thinking, have contributed to his insights on Reality, Ancient History, Christianity, and the Human Condition. His works represent a speculative fusion of style – one that will both entertain and inform readers of all ages.

Crystal Sea Press website: http://www.crystalseapress.com
Crystal Sea Press email: rystalse@crystalseapress.com
Amazon Author Page:
   https://www.amazon.com/author/crystalseapress_enbrown
Goodreads Profile Page:
   https://www.goodreads.com/author/show/19232863.Edward_N_Brown
Facebook Publisher Page:
   https://www.facebook.com/Crystal-Sea-Press-106797100691990/

Other Books by Edward N Brown

The Passion of Thecla: Faith and Fortitude
- 2020 Edition

The Passion of Eve: Remembering the End
- 2020 Edition

The Passion of Eve: Remembering the Beginning
- 2020 Revised Edition

The Passion of Eve: Remembering the Beginning
- 2019 Original Edition

(all books available in Paperback and e-Book formats)

"I AM the ALPHA and the OMEGA," says the Lord God,
"the One who is and who was and who is to come,
the Almighty!"
"I AM the ALPHA and the OMEGA, the First and the Last,
the Beginning and the End!
Blessed are they who wash their robes so as to have free
access to the Tree of Life ..."

Revelation 1:8 and 22:13-14